RELENTLESS

A MEMOIR

JULIAN EDELMAN

WITH TOM E. CURRAN

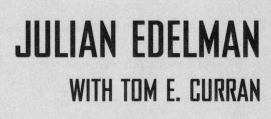

hachette
BOOKS

NEW YORK   BOSTON

Hachette Books
Hachette Book Group
1290 Avenue of the Americas
New York, NY 10104
hachettebookgroup.com
twitter.com/hachettebooks

First Edition: September 2017

Hachette Books is a division of Hachette Book Group, Inc.
The Hachette Books name and logo are trademarks of Hachette Book Group, Inc.

The publisher is not responsible for websites (or their content) that are not owned by the publisher.

The Hachette Speakers Bureau provides a wide range of authors for speaking events. To find out more, go to www.hachettespeakersbureau.com or call (866) 376-6591.

Print book interior design by Timothy Shaner, NightAndDayDesign.biz

Library of Congress Control Number: 2017950936

ISBNs: 978-0-316-47985-1 (hardcover), 978-0-316-47984-4 (ebook)

Printed in the United States of America

LSC-W

10 9 8 7 6 5 4 3 2 1

JULIAN EDELMAN:

FOR MY MOM, DAD, SISTER, BROTHER,
AND THE NEWEST MEMBER OF OUR FAMILY, LILY.

TOM E. CURRAN:

FOR ERICA AND ALL THE TEACHERS, NURSES,
AND COACHES THAT DEDICATE THEIR LIVES
TO HELPING PEOPLE GET BETTER.

CONTENTS

I CAUGHT IT!

From the moment we got into our locker room at halftime, I told anyone who'd listen how the second half was going to go. "It's gonna be a helluva story, boys!"

With the score leaving us buried under a 21–3 deficit, Super Bowl LI had been a thirty-minute horror show at NRG Stadium in Houston. The Atlanta Falcons' speed and execution and our lack of precision put us in a Super Bowl hole deeper than one any team had ever climbed out of.

What made me so sure there would be a plot twist? Didn't I have doubts? No. We'd been in holes like this before. In Super Bowl XLIX, we trailed by 10 at the start of the fourth quarter against Seattle. No team had ever erased a double-digit deficit in the fourth quarter of a Super Bowl. We did.

Nobody believed in us then. I was sure nobody believed in us now. That didn't matter. Nobody believed a lot of us would even get to the NFL. Here we were. Nobody believed Tom Brady would go from a sixth-round pick to the best ever. He did. Nobody believed Bill Belichick was a legend-in-waiting when he was hired by the Patriots in 2000. He was. Nobody believed I could play quarterback at a Division 1 football program in college and turn myself into a wide receiver in the NFL. I had. Our organization was loaded with people who ignored doubters to get where they were.

The key to achieving isn't looking at the ultimate goal. It's believing and then focusing completely on the next step in front of you. That's what our offensive coordinator, Josh McDaniels, kept telling us. "Don't do anything you can't do. Don't try to make it all up in one play. Play each play by itself."

Just before the second-half kickoff, Tom sat down next to me on our bench. I reminded him once more, "Gonna be a helluva story."

"Hell, yeah," he said.

Coming out of halftime, the Falcons threw one more shovelful of dirt on us and went up 28–3. Finally, it was time to dig out, and everybody grabbed a shovel.

We were down 28–9 after three quarters thanks to a James White touchdown catch. We added on a Stephen Gostkowski field goal to make it 28–12. Dont'a Hightower strip-sacked Matt Ryan and TB cashed that in with a touchdown pass to Danny Amendola early in the fourth quarter. We got the two-point conversion from James and you couldn't help but do the math in your head and think, *Hey, we have an opportunity here . . .*

We were almost out of the hole.

There was an excitement right then that you could feel. It's hard to describe it. I've been on mentally tough teams, but this one was something special. We played the first four games of the season without Tom. We lost his backup Jimmy Garoppolo in the second game of the season. We pulled together as a team after getting rocked by the trade of one of our best defensive players, Jamie Collins. We kept on after losing our great tight end Rob Gronkowski to a back injury. We knew how to take a punch. We also knew how to respond to one.

Poise meant everything. We knew what we were in the midst of doing in that second half. Hell, Duron Harmon, one of our safeties, walked into the locker room at halftime and said, "This is going to be the greatest comeback of all time!" and we all believed him. But we had a lot to do to make Duron—and me—prophets. There was no early celebrating. I thought, *It's happening, but I won't get excited like we accomplished something. Just keep going.* One play at a time. Do your job. Stay in the moment. The messages we'd received from Coach Belichick since we became Patriots were in full effect as we took the field with 3:36 remaining, 91 yards and a two-point conversion from tying the game.

We know situations. Our percentages were low. Real low. We had to be almost perfect. We needed a chunk play: a bunch of yards in one big bite. That's important for a successful two-minute drive, and the Falcons knew it as well as we did. They'd be looking for any downfield throws.

On first-and-10 from our 36 with 2:28 left, we went for the chunk.

As we came to the line, I saw that the Falcons' alignment gave me a "chute" route, which meant that if their two safeties were split, I would keep my route thin, sprinting in a direct line toward the goalpost upright nearest me. If there was a single safety in the middle of the field, it would be a situation known as "middle field closed" and I would run a crossing route. It's a pretty standard NFL route. You just adjust and take what the defense is giving you.

Atlanta moved into a defense known as "cover-5." That's two deep safeties, each one covering half of the field, and man-to-man coverage underneath. My defender, the Falcons' corner Robert Alford, had inside leverage, meaning he was lined up to stop me from going inside him to the middle of the field. We both knew that the deep middle was the weak spot, because the safeties were split. Just beat Alford, then get inside him.

We'd executed the same play a couple of times in practice leading up to the Super Bowl back when we were in Foxborough. Usually, if we hit something in practice that's a chunk play, Tom will want to run it because it means we're already comfortable with it. You need that confidence.

Alford was backed off the line about three yards. Our big tight end, Martellus Bennett, was lined up to my right, and outside him was James White, our running back. At the snap, I had to get up on Alford fast, then shake him.

Alford is a really good cornerback—he even had a pick-6 on Tom in the first half—but I felt I had him where I wanted him. I took off hard to set him up for a sharp cut about ten yards downfield. But I didn't give him a great move. Instead of sticking my right foot in the ground hard and cutting sharply, I rushed and rolled into my cut. I didn't get across his face as effectively as I wanted. Alford warded me off and caused me to drift a little farther upfield so my cut wasn't sharp at all.

On a route like this, the quarterback's worst nightmare is the defensive back turning his head around getting a look at the ball, especially if the receiver is behind the DB. That's what Alford did. I saw his head turn and thought, *Oh, shit. If this gets picked, we're done.*

He was slightly off stride, though, so all he could do was jump and bat at it. I jumped when he did, so I was stuck in the air, staring at the ball as it dropped. I was like a guy in the desert who hasn't seen water in ten days pulling up to a stream. I had to get to that ball. It felt like life or death.

Alford was on the ground now, the ball falling toward him. The two safeties—Ricardo Allen and Keanu Neal—weren't split anymore. They were coming for the ball, too. I landed, took two little steps to gather myself, and dove, my eyes glued to the ball.

I had to grab it before it dropped to Alford. Neal was pushing through my right side, stretching his hands past mine. The red gloves of Allen were sliding in. Everybody's hands were converging.

The ball hit Alford's leg and I curled my right hand around it at the same time, then repositioned quickly for a better grip with both hands. Alford kicked at the ball. I let go to reposition my hands a second time, then slapped them back on. Now that I had control, I rolled to box out Neal. The critical thing? Neal's arm. I was worried he'd knife his hand in and pry my arm or hand off the ball. That is a huge coaching point for both sides, offense and defense. Whenever there's a contested catch, the defense goes for your arms and rips. All I was thinking was, "Catch and protect, because these MFers are pros! They'll get it loose!"

With Neal digging and me rolling, I realized it never hit the ground. It was time to sell it. Before the referees got to us, I started to yell, "*I caught it! I caught it! I caught it!*" The sales job was important because if the referees ruled that it was incomplete, we would have to challenge the call.

That was risky, because if we didn't win the challenge, we'd lose a time-out. Would it be worth doing that for a twenty-three-yard gain with two minutes left in the game? Whatever the call is, "indisputable video evidence" is needed to overturn it, so we needed the initial ruling to be that it was a catch.

The officials ruled that it was. Now Atlanta had to challenge.

As I stood there, looking up at the video board, I had no doubt that I'd managed to keep the ball off the ground. One of the Falcons' corners, Brian Poole, said, "No way!" And I said to him, "I swear to God! Watch!" It was like we were in a giant living room watching a game together while the game itself was still going on. Weird.

Then we heard the ruling. The catch was upheld. We had our chunk play. We had momentum. And soon, we finished off one helluva story.

Helping the Patriots win another Super Bowl, my second, was an incredible feeling, and that play just about sums up my career. Having to fight. Having to compete against multiple guys when the odds were stacked against me. Having people doubt me. All of it is like gas in my tank.

When I was a kid, I loved stories about guys who overcame, whether it was *Brian's Song* or the Rocky movies or hearing about Joe Montana, a third-round pick who went on to become one of the greatest ever for my hometown 49ers. Any story in which someone was overcoming adversity, I identified with. And all along the way, those stories have been motivators for me. They gave me the mind-set to always be relentless.

I've been told that my story has a lot of the same elements. Going into high school, I was less than five feet tall and didn't even weigh a hundred pounds soaking wet. By my senior year, I was quarterback for my Woodside (California) High School team and we went 13-0. And it has been that way at every level since: junior college, college, and the NFL. Every time something was blocking my path, I had to find a way around it. Or through it. And I've been able to. Not by myself, either. Every success I've had has been shared with my family, because they built the foundation for me. And the coaches, teammates and friends, they all have a part in this, too.

If you find your talent in life (mine just happened to be playing football) and you also have a passion for it and you work hard consistently, there is a very good chance you will realize your dreams. That's been my experience. You can't say you want to do it. You can't talk about it with your friends. You have to do it. You can't just give it a shot and go halfway.

Sometimes it means not finding balance in life. You might not be the best friend. You might not be the best family member who's there all the time. But it was instilled in me from a young age that if you want to be great at something, you have to go after it. Completely. Some people may be able to reach the top on sheer talent, but not a lot of us.

Have you ever heard of FoMO? It's the Fear of Missing Out. A lot of people look at something they want to do with their lives and then look at what it will take to achieve it, and they decide the commitment isn't worth it. People are often too conservative to take that leap of faith.

When I trained for my pro day after finishing at Kent State, it was the one time in my life where I had to be at my absolute best. Everything was riding on how I did. Everything that came before, back to when I was a little kid playing Pop Warner, and everything that could come after rode on it. Would I be an NFL player or would I need to find a post-college job as a firefighter or work next to my dad at A1 Auto Tech? I attacked it like my life was a *Rocky* montage.

When it was time to make the Patriots, of course I had butterflies, of course I had fear of failure, but you have to realize that those things are true in any competition. Fight or flight. You have to embrace it. If you fail, you fail. I've failed plenty of times in my life, more times than I've succeeded. But that's the reality of trying to accomplish something.

And the other thing? In order to achieve, you have to be willing to be pushed by the people who are trying to help you get to where you want to go. People can't get yelled at anymore. A lot of people back down and quit when they get pushed. I understand how society views it these days, but I believe that sometimes as a kid, you need to be called out and told hard truths. You need to be shown the consequences of what will happen if you screw up. You need people who won't say, "Everything's OK . . ." when it really isn't. My father pointed out the bad more than the good. And Coach Belichick spends a lot more time telling us what we need to further improve on instead of patting us on the ass for something we're supposed to be doing anyway.

You have to have thick skin in this world. Look at Barack Obama. All politics aside, this man defied every expectation in becoming the first African American president. All the things he overcame to do that, all he had to endure coming from where he did? I have so much respect for that journey. Or a woman who becomes a CEO or high-level executive in an industry in which women haven't been a part of the plan. She'll hear the doubters, too.

Or a single mom of three deaf children living in Oklahoma who moved cross-country to California so those kids could get an education and not be pushed to the side. Or a guy without a father and no real supervision who lived in a dozen different places growing up, including a trailer park, yet still developed a work ethic and resilience strong enough to build a business and provide for his family. That's what I saw growing up. I've seen the hard route taken.

That single mom? She is my grandmother Mary Louise Hinds. And that guy who grew up like a wild child? He is my dad, Frank Edelman.

It was people like them who taught me to never give up. I mentioned I grew up small—I was four foot eleven and ninety-five pounds in ninth grade, to be exact—and I wanted to play in the NFL. If I looked in the mirror every day and tried to picture myself playing in the NFL at that size, I would have found a great way to be discouraged.

But I wasn't thinking then how to beat an NFL defender, because, well, what's the point? If you're focused on that distant goal, you're missing what's right in front of you, and that's what you can control. If you're doing everything else in your life fundamentally sound, and you're identifying weaknesses and you're working consistently hard to improve those, you're on the right path.

And when someone tells you that you can't do it? You use it as fuel. You play games with yourself. You create a story and you make yourself the hero.

You hear shit all the time but, at the end of the day, when you're working on your craft, you're not thinking about the negativity. That may get you started, but you can't stop in the middle of practice and say, "Damn, this guy thinks I'm too slow. Or too small . . ." The motivation has to come from somewhere inside you, and you have to grow it.

You have to outlast the doubters. Because it gets hard. Then it gets harder. And a lot of people don't like it. They don't like the pressure in their chest. But I thrive on it, the feeling that it's on me.

For anyone out there who is surrounded by doubters, I hope you find some inspiration in my story. I still have a lot of football in me, but getting here has been a wild ride, and I have aspired to be nothing if not relentless.

TWO

NO SNIVELING!

Why do I like that pressure in my chest? Why do I like it when it's all on me? Why am I the way I am? We all wonder that. And we usually come back to the same place: it's where we grew up and who we grew up with.

Any challenges that I've had to face, I know that my mom, Angie, and my pops, Frank, faced even greater ones when they were growing up and while raising me, my brother, Jason, and my sister, Nicki. Their message was loud and clear: it's supposed to be hard. Life's not easy. It wasn't easy for them, and it wasn't going to be easy for us.

I'm going to tell you some stories about my dad and me. Let's just say his methods for making me a better athlete were . . . unconventional. Definitely not what you'd find in a parenting handbook. But everything came from a place of love. Always. He must have told us a million times, "No sniveling." That means no feeling sorry for yourself. He'd tell us there was nothing we couldn't do if we worked hard enough but he'd also tell us what "real" hard work was. My dad was living proof of that.

I grew up in Redwood City, California, about a half hour south of San Francisco, twenty-five minutes north of San Jose. It's located where Silicon Valley begins, not really a "city" city—there's about 75,000 people living there—and it has a motto you'll love: "Climate Best by Government Test." Catchy, right? That's up on an archway as you enter downtown, inspired by some study pre–World War I that declared Redwood City, the Canary Islands, and the Mediterranean coast of North Africa had the best climates in the world. I don't know about that, but we did have a lot of nice days.

It's pretty diverse socioeconomically. There are really nice parts and there are areas that are middle- and lower-income. It's changed a lot since I was a kid since the tech industry blew up. In these hills overlooking San Francisco Bay, dozens of companies have popped up and taken on the world, with names like Oracle, Electronic Arts, and Shutterfly, all of which are based in Redwood City. Real estate prices have gotten pretty ridiculous because of the boom.

Take the house I grew up in, at 1154 Oliver Street. Three bedrooms and two bathrooms and 1,800 square feet. Today, it would list for about $1.25 million. Frank and Angie paid $186,000 for it right after I was born in 1986. Even the trailer homes across the tracks by the highway, where my dad was living when he met my mom, are now worth over $200,000.

Besides being between San Fran and San Jose, Redwood City is also right between Palo Alto and San Mateo, where Tom Brady grew up. Door-to-door from Oliver Street to the Bradys' house on Portola Drive is less than nine miles. But we'll talk more about him later.

Growing up, I thought of our town as hard-nosed and diverse. San Carlos and Menlo Park were next door and a little ritzier, and the kids were pretty much cut from the same cloth. Redwood City had Samoans, Tongans, Mexicans, a few black kids, and your tough white kids from East Redwood City, where I was raised until my family moved to Highland Avenue in 1997.

It was really a great place to be a kid. I grew up across from Red Morton Park on Roosevelt Street, and that's where we did everything: Pop Warner, Little League, softball, skateboarding, birthday parties. It was perfect for me. Our family did everything together there.

Like I said, Redwood City when I grew up wasn't like it was now. And Redwood City in 1960, when my dad was born? Different place. Frank didn't have quite the same Redwood City experience that I and my siblings had. And that's probably why, even though Redwood City has become kind of affluent, we always had that hard-nosed working-class mind-set.

My dad's only memory of his father, John Harry Edelman, is of looking down on him in his casket in August of 1964 when my dad was three years old. Frank was the only child that my grandmother, Mary Hinds, had with John. His sisters and brother—Mae, Karlyn, and Jeff—were all more than ten years older than Frank and were products of my grandma's first marriage. The three kids were all deaf.

In Oklahoma, where Mary lived in the late '40s and early '50s with her husband, things weren't as progressive and inclusive as they are now. When you were deaf, you were described as "deaf and dumb." Mary's husband in Oklahoma wanted to put Mae, Jeff, and Karlyn in an asylum. Mary wasn't having that.

She looked for institutions that catered to the deaf and found the California School for the Deaf in Berkeley. So Mary packed up the Rambler one day and moved to Hayward, California, just across the bay from Redwood City, and registered her kids in the school.

Mary and John married in 1960, and my dad showed up that year. Dad never got to know John before he died, so Mary tried again and again to find father figures for Frank. If someone was nice to my dad and the deaf kids, they were in. If they were mean, they were out. As a result, Mary got married a few times, and there was a lot of moving around.

My grandmother was a really hardworking and loving lady. She worked two jobs to keep things going, and that kind of love and work ethic she passed down to my dad, no question. Think about the courage she showed back in the 1950s and 1960s, and the sacrifice she made for her kids to get them where they needed to be. It really amazes me.

But with her working and my aunts and uncle being so much older, my dad didn't have a lot of supervision. While he was as close as he could be to his brother and sisters— he actually learned sign language before he learned how to speak—they were away at school at Berkeley for much of the year, so my dad was on his own quite a bit from a young age.

For Frank, every day was like *Home Alone*. He was almost totally responsible for himself, which he says wasn't that abnormal back in his day. After he woke up and had his breakfast, he'd be out the door, then would find a friend and be either on foot or on his Royce Union bike, pedaling around the east side of Redwood City, where his family moved in 1964.

Frank Edelman

My mother would say, "Frankie, you could do anything you want if you work hard."

As long as she had her vodka and her ciggys, she was happy and would love you to death. She was the type that would massage your feet after a twelve-hour day or hear you come in at two a.m. and wake up saying, "Honey, you sit down and I'll make you something to eat." That kind of mom.

My mom went out a lot. She used to give directions around town completely by using bars. You'd say, "Mom, how do you get to the store?" She'd say, "Well, you take a left at the Glo-Worm, take a right at the Rendez-Vous, go all the way down to the Gold Cage and then right along there, you'll find that place, honey." All in the Oklahoma accent. That was my mom.

When I was around eight, she'd bring me with her to the bars on Saturday or Sunday. She'd go in and I'd go out in the alley in the back with my baseball glove and a tennis ball. I played nine-inning games against the wall while my mom was in there having a cocktail. Or I'd take my Nerf football and a hairspray cap, which I used as a tee to kick my football off the walls.

I did try to play Pop Warner at one point. Must have been '70 or '71, and my buddies and I rode our bikes over to Red Morton Park to try out. We showed up with our long hair and who knows what kind of shoes and pants, but I'm just a tiny little kid. After two days, Frank Guida—the coach in charge— comes over and says, "Boys, take a knee."

We're like, "Yeah! We made the team! This is so cool!" Instead, Frank says, "Boys, time to go home. This isn't for you." That's kind of the way it was back in those days. We were the hoods. Showed up, no parents, just running around. I think I was heartbroken a little bit, but we shrugged and moved on.

I remember a basketball court one of our

landlords made for me on Second Avenue and how I'd shoot free throw after free throw out there. I also was playing some baseball and getting pretty good at that. But I was just like Jules, so small. I was born in November, so that late birthday meant I was very young for my grade, and I was small to begin with.

My brother Jeff was ten years older than me and a real good football player at the School for the Deaf, and he taught me how to catch. And it's funny because I have these like really skilled hands and fingers, and you know why? Sign language! My fingers and hands were all about sign language. So I got that soft touch all from sign language.

I was so little and I was so fast, like Julian, but I had no coaching and no team, really. I could compete, no problem, but I wasn't the best. One day I noticed that the guys who were the best had their dads coaching them and showing them what to do. I was like "Damn, man. If I would have had a dad, I would be right with those guys."

Finally, when I was in seventh grade, my mom met a guy named Walt Kronquist. He was really good to me and he was the dad I was looking for at that time. And Mary liked him, too.

First year of high school and I was on the football team. That was my only time I ever played tackle football. I was this little baby out there but I was pretty good. Still fast, but small. There used to be this thing they would do after the game for kids who didn't play. It was called the "fifth quarter" and we'd go out there and get some plays. So in the second game I played, I'm playing cornerback and I'm covering a guy in the end zone and the quarterback just throws it right over my head for a touchdown. I ran off that field crying. I failed. And that was the end of my football career.

I wished I had someone there when I walked off that field to push me back on. There's a moment in people's lives when you need support and you need encouragement. You need someone to say, "It's OK, you'll get better at it." Or that push. Now, my mom supported me and told me I could do anything I wanted to. But sometimes you need masculine support. Support from a father. And I was going to make sure that my kids weren't going to miss out on that.

Soon after my dad let up that touchdown, he and Grandma moved in with Walt and Dad enrolled at Fremont High. So you see where this is headed, right? My dad is out of sports and into work. And somewhere down the road, somebody was going to get all that coaching Dad never had. And then some.

In the meantime, Frank had an incredible work ethic. By fourteen, he had a job at a Shell gas station. Dad took it seriously, getting his certifications and really moving up the ranks throughout high school. Meanwhile, he had two auto shop teachers at Fremont who let him be the teaching assistant. That meant he could be in shop class pretty much all day. My dad was king of auto shop. He got a lot of Cs and Ds in everything else, but not shop. He was passing and he was learning a trade.

That's the thing about Pops. He always has to be working, always has to be moving forward. He's not a great relaxer; even though he takes a nap every day at some point, that's just a recharge. Either he's earning money or getting smarter or trying to get better. He doesn't do things just to do things.

In Dad's last year of high school, Grandma left Walt. It was tough all around. Walt was in so many ways exactly what Dad needed at that time. Some structure and that father figure. But Dad had grown up so much. He wasn't the same little greaser. He was a man now, in a lot of ways. He had a trade and was graduating high school.

Meanwhile, my dad met a girl named Angie Gole.

I'm a lot like my mom. A little loud, a little playful. Rascals. That's what my dad calls us. Like me, my mom is a middle child. She was born in Canada—Kitchener, Ontario—in 1960. Her parents were Germans who lived in Belgium before emigrating to Canada. She has a brother, Peter, and a sister, Connie.

Her father, my Opa, was a bricklayer named Mathias, and my Oma was named Isolde. Opa moved to Redwood City in 1963 by himself in his red Volkswagen bug with $200 in his pocket. After he got an apartment on Hess Road and saved some money, he sent for Oma, my mom, and Peter.

All the room and freedom my dad had growing up? My mom was completely at the other end of the spectrum, with strict rules. She had to lie and sneak around just to go to a party or a dance. My Oma made Mom's clothes until she was about eighteen. I think that's why Mom loves shopping so much now. But it was really tough for her. They had no family—all the relatives are back in Belgium, even now—so it was the five of them surviving on their own.

My Opa was a tough, strong man. They say I get my power from him, though my dad's got some old-man strength, too. Opa worked and saved until he'd put away $17,000, which was enough to buy a house on C Street. In cash.

My mom told stories about how she was the fastest girl in the eighth grade. She did some gymnastics at school, too, but other than that she didn't do much in the way of activities. Her parents really didn't know where to guide her, and she was very sheltered. "Zees ees not how vee do tings" was a phrase she heard a lot growing up.

Her upbringing was different from my dad's. But as sheltered as she was, Angie was fearless, too. When we were kids, we could see she was athletic, like when we went out to our lake house and went waterskiing. She could slalom on a single ski, no problem. I realize it now when I'm going on dates. I'll meet other girls, and think, *Man, my mom was kind of a little badass!*

My mom and I are partners in crime, and that could drive Pops a little crazy. We both love our clothes, and when I was young my mom would feed that. I remember the summer before my freshman year of high school: It was the first time in years I wasn't in private school and wouldn't be wearing a uniform, so my mom took me shopping and she went all out. We bought maybe five outfits, two pairs of shoes, and I thought, "Holy smokes! This is like Christmas or Hanukah!" Dad got home and said, "Angie, we can't do this!" But she'd always take the heat for us.

The thing about my mom, she never thought she wasn't young. When I was a kid she'd be listening to Red Hot Chili Peppers or rapping along with Snoop. She was always cool. She still is.

THREE

BAM-BAM ARRIVES

After high school when she was nineteen, Angie married a man named Ron Rodriguez and had my brother, Jason. Ron and Mom shared the same circle of friends with Frank, and my dad once actually loaned them his Trans Am.

It didn't take too long for Mom to realize that she and Ron had different visions for how life was going to be. She was so young and hadn't really experienced life. She always says, "I was still such a baby at that time." Two years into their marriage, they divorced and Mom moved back in with her parents. By then, Mom and Dad had become close friends. Dad was really into her. And he loved Jason, too.

Frank, meanwhile, pursued a budding music career when he wasn't working at the Shell station during the day. He started with a local band called Canyon, then moved on to a Top 40 band called Fortune. They played two or three nights a week and on the weekends. As Pops's playing improved, he built a reputation. He jumped to the Kids, which was one of the best bands in the area. Now he was playing up to five nights a week and doing some jazz nights as well.

Dad was balancing the Shell job with the band, but he knew he couldn't do both when the Kids announced they were going on a tour of Japan for forty-five days. By then, Mom was living at home and she and Dad had become a full-blown item. Dad was head over heels for her, but he needed to see how far the music would take him, so he told Bob Witters at the Shell station he was leaving for Japan.

For about eighteen months, including that tour of Japan, Dad chased his dream, and got a feel for what the life was like. They opened for some great acts—Journey, Huey Lewis, Marty Vallee, the Tubes—but the band politics, the schedule, and the partying just weren't his thing. When they got back from Japan, Dad realized that it was time to jump off that ship. The other guys were lifelong musicians. Dad wasn't in it like they were. So about three months after they came back from Japan, in late 1981, Dad decided to hang it up. Music career over at twenty-one.

He and Mom moved into an apartment together. Dad sold his Yamaha CP70 keyboard to buy an engagement ring and he asked Mom to marry him. She said yes. Then he went back to work at the Shell station in early 1982, but it was soon sold, and Dad, who had built up a reputation as a mechanic, decided to set up shop at the house. Things went well for a while as people dropped off their cars while Mom served lemonade and shuttled them to work.

When the city came down and informed Dad he couldn't run a repair shop out of his home, he started A-1 Autotech, which he still runs to this day.

Over the next few years, it was just the three of them—Mom, Dad, and Jason–building a business, sinking their roots deeper into the community and creating a family. But whatever peace and quiet they had ended on May 22, 1986. I showed up.

Jason was seven years old when I arrived. It was a tough adjustment for him, going from getting all the attention all the time to me being everywhere.

Jason Rodriguez

I was an only child and life was great. Then Julian came along and I had a little brother and . . . he was a tough kid to deal with. He was a mix between Bam-Bam and the Tasmanian Devil. The kid was just an animal. He tore everything apart. Wherever he went, there was a mess behind him. I remember one time my parents left him with one of their friends so they could take me somewhere. When we picked him up, he had a knot on his head the size of a golf ball. And somehow he'd thrown a glass Coke bottle through their coffee table. He was probably two or three at the time. At the most.

So I liked to have a good time. Actually, it sounds like I was a major pain. I was nine pounds and one ounce of colicky, crying kid when I showed up at the Kaiser hospital in Redwood City. I needed a lot of attention. Some things never change.

My parents told me there was one scary period three months after I was born when I was diagnosed with spinal meningitis. Dad's sister, Aunt Karlyn, had it in the 1950s and it nearly killed her, so Dad was devastated and thinking the worst, but luckily I pulled through and was home within a week.

Having Jason to chase around sped everything up for me. I was walking at nine and a half months and roller skating by two years old. Since I'd invaded Jason's space and wasn't going anywhere, he made the best of it. I became his personal crash test dummy.

The family moved to 1154 Oliver Street when I was two. It was a little square house with three bedrooms and one bathroom in a dense neighborhood. There was a tiny front yard where Mom planted a tree and installed a lawn. There was a backyard that I took full advantage of. Eventually, there was a hoop in the driveway.

Best of all, we were within walking distance of Red Morton Park. When I was growing up, Red Morton seemed to go on forever. There were soccer fields, softball fields, the Little League fields—Mitchell and Kiwanis—and a big baseball diamond called McGarvey. They built an amazing skate park, and there was a gymnasium, playgrounds, and football fields where we practiced Pop Warner. It's impossible to estimate the hours our family spent there. Jason played all the way through Pop Warner for Dad and old Frank Guida. (Remember? The guy who told Dad to hit the road when he tried out for Pop Warner in 1970?) Nicki was a cheerleader, Mom did absolutely everything—concessions, programs, fund-raisers, sales—and Dad eventually became president of Pop Warner and ran the whole thing.

Jason and I shared a bedroom and we were in bunk beds. This was dangerous for me because Jason was into the WWF, so he practiced his wrestling moves on me. We had this giant pillow in our room that he would cover me with, then he'd jump off the top bunk onto me pretending he was coming off the top rope.

Jason Rodriguez

I used to put him on his stomach and give him a wedgie, then I would tie his legs in a backwards figure-four and hook his underwear to it so he couldn't get out. I tormented him pretty bad. He was a pain in the ass but he was fun because we could do anything to him and nothing fazed him. Not even when we'd dress him up in a helmet and shoulder pads and use him as a tackling dummy.

The backyard wasn't big at Oliver Street, but I made the most of it. I was a builder. I loved banging on things, trying to create. My biggest creation was a massive fort connecting the tree house, toolshed, and a smaller fort with a bridge. The small fort was my own space, and Dad made sure the thing was primo. It was just a box, but it had a hinged door for a roof and it was pretty cool. I'm sure Dad built it to code.

My whole family used to call me MacGyver because I was always rigging up some device to do something. I was an active kid. I wanted to be out doing things, not inside playing video games or watching TV. And Mom and Dad wouldn't let us do that anyway.

As Nicki got older, she became caught up in my shenanigans.

Nicki Edelman

I think he forgot I was a girl sometimes because he treated me like a little brother my whole life. There was a lot he did with just his friends but he always included me in stuff, and if no one was around, it would be the two of us. Playing in the street, in the backyard, building with Legos, being in his fort, he was a great big brother. And he was pretty high energy. I mean, I'm an elementary school teacher in

Redwood City now, and I can only imagine the challenges Julian must have brought with his energy. He actually groomed me to be a better teacher because I haven't yet dealt with anyone more high energy than he was.

Julian might have been Jason's crash-test dummy, but I was his. Whatever Jason did to him, Julian definitely tried on me, so I grew up as a tomboy because of that.

Jules was very much the middle child. Outgoing like my mom, always up for something. But Jules also had such a strong personality. When he knew what he wanted, he would do whatever he had to do to get it at all costs. That's been him from day one, which is part of the reason he is where he is. If someone said he couldn't do it, he'd do it on purpose to spite them.

I liked to fix things, too. I'd do things like pull my blue Specialized Fatboy bike apart and put it back together for the fun of it. Bikes were big, and I would cruise around the neighborhood with my buddies Kurt De La Rosa, Scottie Bassett, and Jeff Belluomini, finding something to do whether it was basketball, hitting dirt jumps, line ball, skateboarding, whatever.

When we weren't playing sports we were out in the woods getting poison oak, cuts and bruises on our bikes. There were no cell phones, so you'd go out the door and say, "Hey, I'm going to Kurt's!" and the answer would be "All right, be back for supper!" and we'd be out there for the entire day.

Dad worked so hard when we were young that when he came home, we all wanted to be around him. Any project he had going on around the house, I'd try to get involved in. I remember putting up Christmas lights one year. I was real young, maybe nine years old. I got to go on the roof with him. I always loved doing the crazy shit. Heights and speed. Anyway, I was supposed to stay in one spot. I remember him saying, "Jules, do not walk over here!" I crawled over to see what he was doing. He let me come up close to him. I remember it was a crisp night and we were lying on the roof just looking up. Really peaceful. Then he took a dead bulb, and he threw it into the street and it made a big pop. Then he let me do it. That was pretty cool.

We built a retaining wall together when I was young. That was a lot of work. But Jason, as the oldest, had to do a lot more of the hard labor than I did. Over time, I got most of the fun stuff.

I loved going to the shop, too. In 1992, Dad moved A-1 Auto Tech from West Evelyn to the place he's been now for the past twenty-five years: Pioneer Way in Mountain View. I actually bought the building in 2011, so I'm his landlord now, but when I was real young I'd be out there in the parking lot pounding away on junk cars. I'd bring my skateboard and when I was older, my car, which I'd wax and clean. I'd help out Dad when I could, too.

One thing I had to have was a go-kart. I asked for one after the movie *Heavy Weights* came out, and finally, when I was eleven, Dad bought it. We would pack it in his old pickup and go to Cañada College where there was an area with a pile of tires. I would do donuts and fly around those tires, and I was always looking for Dad's approval. I would say, "How was that, Dad, getting sideways there?" And he would tell me what adjustments I needed to make.

I went to Roosevelt from kindergarten through fourth grade. It was a little rough, a scrappy school, and my parents decided that they wanted me to start going to private school, so we applied to Our Lady of Mount Carmel in Redwood City. I tested as a C student for my grade so I was held back a year going in, because the transition from public to private was seen as a big jump. I wasn't too happy about it. I was suddenly the held-back kid in private school repeating fourth grade, and I was small. Pops kept saying, "Son, it's all going to work out." He always had a master plan. He could see that I was going to be like him: small and having to prove myself all the way through.

FOUR

INTO THE FOOTBALL FIRE

When Jason turned eight, Dad signed him up for Redwood City Pop Warner. Naturally, Pops got involved. At first, he was on the periphery as a coach, learning the game from a technical standpoint. But Dad being Dad, he took it seriously and attacked coaching football like he attacked learning piano or fixing cars.

After a couple of years spent helping, he became a position coach and began attending seminars on different offensive and defensive schemes. There were some really good coaches at that level to help Dad figure it out, so he took advantage of it.

The Redwood City Pop Warner 49ers was no bullshit. This wasn't a youth football program that rolled out the balls and kicked up dirt for a couple of hours. Coach Guida was a hard-ass. Coach Guida's son, Ed coached Jason in Pee Wees. He was the same way. There was yelling and swearing, and there were tears. Pop Warner was truly tougher than high school football. There were expectations.

Frank Edelman

Redwood City was in the elite level. It wasn't like, "OK, we're just gonna go to Pop Warner and we're gonna be lame and we're gonna get beat and everybody just have a good time." That wasn't this group. That wasn't Redwood City. There were other leagues that may have been a little less competitive in the area. That was fine, you could choose to go there. But if you were signing up in Redwood City, you knew what to expect.

Jason was a running back, receiver, safety, and corner. I was there every day at practice from the time I was still in diapers. Jason tells me I spent my early time rummaging through equipment bags on the sideline during practices, emptying out water bottles, throwing stuff around, and generally acting like a little troublemaker.

The time I was spending on the sidelines would make a difference when I was old enough to play.

Jason Rodriguez

I could see his fearlessness as soon as he could walk. Whatever we told him to do, he'd do it.

I remember seeing how athletic he was at four and five years old or at our practices. The coaches, they couldn't wait to get him up on those teams. It was obvious what a terror he was going to be.

He got a couple years' head start learning the playbook. Dad would have us out there in the front yard at Oliver Street running plays out of the

Wishbone. We'd be out there running 21-dive, 33-blast, 45-power, 36-power. And Jules ran them right. He was a pretty amazing little kid.

In 1992, Jason finished Pop Warner and was soon headed off to Saint Francis High School in Mountain View.

Dad took over as head coach of the Pee Wees when I joined the Junior Pee Wees in 1994. That's when he really cranked up his coaching intensity. He was watching film four, five, six hours a night and scouting on Saturdays. He'd drive a hundred miles to go watch a team play. He'd film them himself, then come home and break it down. One of our rivals was Oak Grove. Dad would get there early, find a place in the stands, and tape their pregame to see what they were doing. And this was normal for Pop Warner in our area!

Dad became Pop Warner president and, with Frank Guida as the godfather of the program, he and the other volunteers built the program up to five teams of thirty-two kids each and five cheerleader squads.

Pop Warner eligibility is based on age and weight, and weekly weigh-ins are held to make sure kids aren't turning into giants. Those kids who were near or over the weight, they'd be out there running, sweating, dieting, cutting weight for their weigh-ins. There was total commitment from the families. They loved it. It was a real introduction for kids to hard work, sacrifice, and discipline. For some parents, too.

I have buddies who can still remember the songs Dad would make up to help us remember our blocking assignments: "Head up to play side, but if he's in the gap, you block that gap unless it's a trap!" He made it fun, but everyone was terrified of my father. Along with Ed Guida, he was the scary guy. To this day, if I go to a local bar back home, a guy will come up to me who Dad coached and tell me the same story about how Dad would go up to him, grab his face mask and yell at them with a wad of dip in his lip, dip spraying everywhere. But they loved it because he cared for the kids and did everything he thought was best.

He'd pick up the kids who didn't have rides. He was the equipment guy, too. Everybody respected him, but there's no denying they were scared of him, too.

Kurt De La Rosa

The reason Julian and I became such good friends when we were young was that my mom, Christine, was diagnosed with cancer. At the same time, both my parents were going to school to get their degrees and they were working. Frank basically said, "Hey, Guy [my Dad] and Christine, you have a lot on your plates, especially with Christine's situation. I'll take care of Kurt, get him to practice and all that. Don't worry about that stuff." This began during baseball season, so Julian and I became inseparable.

When I heard the house phone ring while trying to do my homework I would think, "Please don't be Frank!" Next thing you know, I'd hear my dad say, "Kurt! Frank's coming to pick you up. You got practice in five minutes! You guys are going to hit ground balls at such and such field!" I'd think, "Shit!" I knew one or both of us were going to end up crying and one or both of us were going to end up bleeding. So we would go and practice ground balls and Frank would be ripping them at us. He would always be pushing us to be better than what we expected, no room for complacency. All the while he's ripping these shots at us we're terrified but trying to joke and keep our spirits up. One time, I remember I got a bad hop, smashed me right in the face. My nose starts bleeding and I'm like "Ugh, this sucks!" Frank's like, "All right, we'll call it for today." I'm like "How am I supposed to get home, Frank? I'm like bleeding!" He says, "Ride your bike home, you're fine."

It was tough love from Frank, but if he hadn't cared he wouldn't have been out there all those days hitting us ground balls and spending his extra time away from the shop or away from work or away from his family to push us as kids not just in sports but also in life.

Jules took it in stride. He loved sports, he loved competing, and it was in his blood from birth basically because of Frank. I'm out there playing sports, having fun, enjoying the day, looking at the clouds, and Frank would always try to get me out of "la-la land" as he would call it. Julian actually focused as a little kid. He trusted his coach and his coach happened to be his dad, and so it really worked out for him in becoming tougher and getting more than he would expect out of himself.

We'd all see how hard Frank was with Julian. As an adult, you can pass judgment and say, "I don't think this is right." I'll probably do it when I have kids and see other parents coaching; I'll be skeptical of decisions other people make with their kids. But as kids, we looked to adults for our answers and guidance, and we definitely respected our parents and especially Frank and the way he coached us.

You never really question it. You would bitch and moan, but if he said, "We're practicing tomorrow morning," as you're about to go home for dinner, you're like, "All right, well, I don't like it, I want to sleep, but, you know, I'm going to be here on time to practice." That's the way it was.

Kurt thought Dad was a maniac. All my friends thought he was crazy. There'd be people walking by the ballpark, looking at us like, "What the hell?!" They'd say, "Man, your dad yells at you and you yell right back." It was how we did it. I think it was fun. I developed a thick skin, so that whenever anyone else yelled at me, I could let it roll off. I also developed a real work ethic and an understanding that there's a point where practice can be counterproductive. And it did get counterproductive. Especially with baseball. Always with baseball.

The tension would be bubbling when we were in the car heading to the field. It was always over hitting. Fielding? We could do that forever. But with hitting, once I started to be able to hit it out, all I wanted to do was hit bombs. Two strikes? Runner on third, less than two outs? Didn't matter. I was swinging as hard as I could and trying to lift and pull the ball. Dad would be out there saying, "Keep your hands inside the ball! You're trying to lift and pull everything!" One day, I don't know what I did, but Dad was whipping balls at me while I ran around inside the backstop. A couple of his friends saw him and they said, "Hey, Frank, saw you throwing balls at your kid." He didn't care. Neither did I. That's how we did it. That's what we knew.

It always got to the point where we'd both leave upset and we were never coming back, then *bam!* next day, we're back.

There were a couple of times I'd walk home from Red Morton, pissed off, crying. Or he'd hear me chirp back under my breath and he'd throw harder and I'd swing harder and try to hit it farther.

When I was fourteen or fifteen we once went over to Sequoia High School to take batting practice before a game. I wasn't hitting very well. Average down, popping up. Dipping my back shoulder all the time. He was throwing inside. I don't even know if he was trying to. I said something and then he threw one that came skidding in and hit my feet when I tried to jump over it. I threw the bat and ran at him full speed and tried to headbutt him. He grabbed my arms and threw me down, gave me the *doink, doink* to the head. He's holding me down, saying "Are you done?!" and I'm trying to headbutt him from the ground. I wasn't done! I split my lip on my new braces and went to the game with a bloody jersey.

With every sport, from day one, I was one hundred miles an hour. My parents signed me up for soccer when I was four (they sneaked me in) and I played that until I was eight. The first thing my coach said was, "You're a tiger!" I embraced that. He gave me something as a little guy to pretend that I was. And it stuck with me. I had that mentality with baseball, but it is more of a skilled sport. You have to be able to focus and really work techniques. And for me, the tough part was hitting. With the glove, no problem. I took pride in that. I loved taking infield before the game because I could get out there and style at shortstop: backhands, diving stops, gunning it across. I also loved running the bases and getting to create a little chaos.

Pops would get mad at me in T-ball because I'd keep running through base coaches, through stop signs, sliding headfirst. It was Dad's fault, though. He told me all about Pete Rose and how he ran everywhere, slid headfirst, took out

Ray Fosse in the 1970 All-Star Game. I figured that's what I should do. Be a tiger.

Dad would always talk about the importance of the mind game. He'd tell me, "If you don't make it, it's because you don't have the mental toughness for it." He'd have my sister, Nicki, out there yelling when I was trying to hit or during a drill, trying to distract me. Then, after a big fight, he'd say, "That's why you're not gonna make it!"

Frank Edelman

I was pretty bad. But I was bad in a good way, if that makes sense. Me and him, in baseball, we would always fight. We practiced literally every single day. It wasn't that I was obsessed about making him a professional athlete. That was never the goal. All I knew was work, head home and say to Jules, "Homework done? Let's go practice." If he was tired, didn't matter. We're going to practice. We went camping every year right after the regular baseball season ended and before football. I had to get him ready for baseball all-stars, so we'd bring the bats and balls and we'd go find a field while camping. We'd take one hundred swings, take one hundred grounders. I did that literally every day of the year. In basketball season, I'd go rent a gym and we'd practice. Then in football, I'd put glasses on him and tape one of the eyes shut to make it harder to see the ball coming. I'd tape up one of his hands or wave my hand in front of his face so he'd have interference and have to concentrate. But he liked it. He'd get mad, we'd fight. Then we'd do it again the next day.

I'm surprised I didn't wreck him. My kids didn't have a normal upbringing. It was all about work. It was all about staying productive. I figured that everything you do has to benefit you. I really wasn't into sitting around and having fun. Everything I did, you were learning or bettering yourself, whether it be baseball, football, basketball, or being with a tutor. He wasn't just hanging out. He had very little free time. I wasn't educated, so I couldn't teach them math and English, so that's why I would hire tutors. I couldn't teach them how to study, because I was a screw-off. I was pretty ignorant. Knowing what the world was like out there, what I saw, what I went through, I was trying to keep them surrounded by good people, not bad people. I'm an East Side boy. It was rough where I grew up. They weren't bad people, but it was rough for a lot of people, with either drugs, booze, crime, no jobs, time on their hands and nothing good ever coming from that. That path was something I avoided. And that path was something I didn't want my kids to see. Of course, once you do all that and put them in parochial schools you find out the same dangers are there, too!

I wanted my kids not to be me. I wanted them to have more than what I had. And the only way I knew how to do it was be a bully and give more yelling than loving. There was plenty of that—"I love you but shut up and get to work." That was kind of normal for our generation.

I remember one time that still bothers me. Jules was playing basketball for Mount Carmel. He was a seventh grader. The play was basically, pass it here, pass it there, pass it to Jules, Jules you shoot. So Jules came home one day and said, "Dad, coach came to me and wants me to go play on the eighth-grade team." I said, "You're not playing on the eighth-grade team. You're staying on the seventh-grade team. You go up to the eighth-grade team, you can't go back down. Stay where you can get time and have fun." He said, "I'm going up." I said, "No, you're not." He said "Dad, I'm going up and that's it." And he makes a move for the stairs, and I grabbed him and said, "YOU ARE STAYING DOWN IN THE SEVENTH GRADE!" At that moment, I felt him collapse a little bit. Melt away from me. He was scared of me. And I didn't like that. It scared me. I broke up a little bit and I just didn't feel good about it. Over something stupid. He was all excited and I crushed that. It felt awful.

Did I overdo it with Jules? Yeah. Jules came out of the womb running. I couldn't break that little guy. I saw it early and he thrived on all of it. And I had to learn on my own how to do it. Being uneducated on how to do any of it, I was just figuring it out as I went. But I knew when I crossed the line.

I don't know if I'll coach my kids the way Dad coached me. It's a different era. I don't think what he did was bad, but the cops would probably be pulling up half the time with Dad if he was out there coaching me like that now! It wasn't like he was kicking my ass, but I don't know if you could do it these days.

Jason and Nicki would say I was the golden child because Pops and I would train and work out so much. He'd do it to my sister but he felt uncomfortable yelling at a girl. She always had my dad by the balls. And Jason had it ten times harder than I did, and he didn't go back at Dad as hard as I did.

I was a little punk, too, and had a way of pushing his buttons. Kurt and I were probably eight years old and I'd gotten a BB gun, so Kurt was spotting for me, trying to find birds to shoot. Of course, I hit one and it landed in the neighbor's yard. He was an old Russian dude and he looked up and Kurt was right next to me. I put the gun behind me but the gun barrel was sticking out over my head. He went, "Did you guys shoot this?" We went, "No! We didn't."

We ran inside and started playing. Then the cops came and took my gun. Kurt went home, and I was so scared of what Dad was going to do. I would get in trouble for getting a C in class, but cops? *Oh my God, I'm going to die.* Mom called Dad and he told me, "I'll be home at three thirty."

The anxiety from that is still fresh. I'd been selected for baseball all-stars, so he gave me a decision that I had to make. "I can give you three licks on the bare butt with a belt," he said. "Or you don't play in the all-star game and not go on the vacation." So I took the belt. But he was so soft. He would come in the room after and he would say, "You know I'm just trying to make you a better man."

Angie Edelman

I always thought he was too tough on him, but Jules loved it. It wasn't like they were running to hide from Frank.

One day I was looking out the window on Oliver Street and he's out there dribbling a basketball up and down the street. I thought, "What a weirdo." I yelled out to him, "What are you doing?" He said, "Dad called and told me to dribble for a half hour." Or he'd be out there shooting in the backyard counting shots. I'd ask, "What are you doing?" He'd answer, "Dad told me to shoot one hundred times." And Jules did it. He loved it as much as Frank did. There was fighting but it wasn't abuse. Frank loved the kids as hard as any father could. And all three kids know that.

FIVE

THE ROAD TO DISNEY WORLD

After all those years watching Jason play and Dad coach the Redwood City 49ers, I was finally old enough to play in the fall of 1994. Junior Pee Wee football, number 44. Which was appropriate because I weighed about forty-four pounds. The minimum weight was fifty pounds, so I was drinking a bunch of water to make weight.

My first year, I was a young buck rookie. We ran the Wishbone offense and I was one of two backs behind the fullback and quarterback. I played the four spot—lined up off the fullback's right butt cheek—where the smaller back usually played. I didn't have a fear of getting hit, because nothing that happened to me out there was worse than what Jason and his buddies did to me back at Oliver Street. I was crash tested.

Being fast was my thing. When I went to Roosevelt Elementary, I was the fastest, then when I went to Mount Carmel, I went in there looking for the fastest kid. His name was Leo Ortiz and I challenged him to a base race. That's when you stand at home plate and run the bases in opposite directions and whoever makes it home first wins. Neither of us made it home. We collided at second base. Anything at Mount Carmel that had to do with sports I was into. The Presidential Fitness Awards and all that, I'd be out there trying to break the records in chin-ups and the mile. I remember the second-fastest person at the school was Liz Shea. She could light it up. Never got me, though!

I never felt completely at home when I was at Mount Carmel. I was an outcast for a long time. I had come from public school, I was repeating fourth grade, I didn't really know any of the kids, I had slicked hair, I was uncomfortable in my uniform, I just didn't like it. It was real classy and I really wasn't. I knew what was expected, but getting detention for having your shirt untucked? This was bullshit. I was a little punk about it and didn't mesh with anyone at all for the first few months.

Cliques broke down according to where you were from and what league you played baseball in. I was from Highlander, which was middle class; Nationals was upper income, and Americans was lower income. A lot of the kids at Mount Carmel were Nationals—I didn't know those kids!

I was most at home with football and my family. Practices usually started at five thirty p.m. Dad left around five to set up the field. He'd set out the tackling dummies and equipment, then perch his big orange Gatorade cooler on the tailgate of our 1991 Chevy Suburban and put the cups out. People knew us by the 'Burban. Big blue and white beast.

Everyone knew the Edelmans, that's for sure. By the time I was twelve, as I mentioned, Dad was president of Pop Warner and the head coach of the Pee Wees. Meanwhile, Mom was running the concessions or the merchandise, Nicki was a cheerleader (she hated it) and Jason, when he wasn't playing for Saint Francis, was helping as an assistant coach.

In 1996, I was ten and it was my third year on Junior Pee Wees. By now, we were getting pretty good. I'd been around the game all my life. I'd been running that Wishbone offense since I was four or five because Dad used to practice with Jason and me at Oliver Street. We were still doing it. We'd line up in the street, Dad using rocks to mark where the linemen would be and he'd be the quarterback and send me out for passes: 45-power pass release, 36-power pass, four-back go. There's actually a video somewhere of us practicing in the street. Thinking about it now, I don't even know why we did it. Maniacs. But it was working, and even though I was small, I was playing linebacker. I knew the ins and outs of the game. I understood it. I knew where blockers were coming from and how to slip them and still get to the ball. On offense, I was becoming a little stud. I had twelve touchdowns in ten games.

Finally, when I was eleven, I got to Dad's team. Now it was more intense. We were a good group and Dad was a really good coach. He knew his shit. At this point, I was turning into a good player. I was fast, quick, I knew how to juke, I always had great vision because I understood the game and could anticipate. I could stop on a dime and cut back. I could spin, always had really good balance.

My on-field personality was starting to take shape, too. I was a little bit of an asshole. I sounded like a little general out there with my team, screaming, "Let's go! We got to get better." I'd been around it for so long and seen the older kids and coaches do that, so it was natural for me. It's a demanding sport and I was comfortable speaking up. I wasn't shy about making play recommendations to the coaches, either. I'd go to the sidelines and yell at Dad, "The guards wide! Let's do a cross or let's do a trap!" Sometimes he'd bitch at me to let him call the plays but, then we'd eventually run it and it would work.

In 1998, we made it to the Pop Warner National Championship at Disney World in Florida. We were pretty advanced for twelve-year-olds, thanks to our coaches. At the line of scrimmage, the offense would know; they wouldn't have to even look at each other. "If we're running 34-power and this guy's on outside shade in the three hole, that's going to kick over to a counter-cross trap." Boom, we run it. Automatically.

I was still only about eighty pounds. But I was faster than anyone else on the team and we were stacked. We were just so much better than everyone. Our line was insanely good and our defense was amazing—we didn't give up a touchdown in the regular season! I had thirty-six touchdowns, and a lot of them were long ones.

We were scheduled for two games in Florida. The first one was against a team from Naperville, Illinois, outside Chicago. They had this running back who was 112 pounds— by the end of the year you could be 112—he was a big old dude, and this team ran the Wing-T to perfection. When this kid ran, he looked like Gronk pulling defenders behind him. They scored on their first drive and missed the extra point (which was worth two points if you kicked). We'd never been punched in the face like that. I remember wondering, "How are kids going to react?" We looked at each other in the huddle like, "Holy shit, what do we have going here?"

Their 6-2 defense was messing up our offense and we were in for a fight. We had to throw. Finally, late in the fourth quarter, we threw a screen to Steven Aros and he went forty yards for the touchdown. We won 8–6 and then faced a team from Texas, the Oak Cliff Redskins.

This team was extremely fast and ridiculously athletic. The kids were running like 4.6 40s at twelve years old. We ended up beating them pretty easily—none of the drama that we had against Naperville.

Everyone was ecstatic, but it was really special for Dad. Here's a guy who'd been told he couldn't play Pop Warner, and now he'd coached his son's team to a national championship. What an accomplishment.

I wore my red Redwood City Niners jacket to Mount Carmel. It had all the patches on it—North County Sectional Champions, National Champions—and it felt awesome. Most of the kids at Mount Carmel didn't really know anything about me and football, though. Those were two different worlds. What I was doing in football was separate from school.

I played two more years of Pop Warner and noticed how the other kids were getting bigger and I wasn't. They were hitting puberty and I still looked like I was eight years old. I wasn't the fastest kid anymore. I was getting left behind.

For a long time, being small didn't make a difference. I was one of the best players on the field so I never thought of it as a disadvantage.

But when I was thirteen years old, everyone was definitely getting taller. I always had girlfriends, but now I was a head shorter than them. It was embarrassing.

I was trained to not look too far ahead in sports. I was too busy going from one season to the next to think about whether I'd be playing in college or professionally someday. But when I did think about it, I was always so pissed off about my size. How could I think about playing in the NFL when I had no clue if I'd ever grow?

Dad says I'd go to him crying at night, asking him, "When am I going to grow?" I don't remember it quite like that, but I did complain about it. I'd always blame Mom and Dad for being so small. I was joking, but not really. I could tell how much it was killing Dad. He taught us that hard work and practice can cover for a lot of things, but being small isn't something you can overcome with effort. You have to have patience. And that's what he'd tell me. "It'll come."

Meanwhile, there were all these little embarrassments. When I got my license, I definitely didn't look old enough to drive. I got pulled over once because of it and I asked the officer to call Mom. He said to her, "Your son straight up looks twelve years old." Mom flipped out about him talking like that in front of me. A big reason I stopped playing baseball for a while was because, when I was fifteen, my summer-league coach practically benched me because he thought I was too small.

Kurt De La Rosa

Jules and I were both the smallest guys on our teams growing up. Going into high school I was four ten, which was right around the same height he was when he went into high school. But freshman year was when I started hitting my growth spurt, so if you take a look at the picture of us from my sophomore year and his freshman year when we were on JV baseball together, I'm already head and shoulders above him in height. He thought he was always going to be the smallest at that point. It didn't matter much in youth sports, because of his quickness and his aggressive-ness as a competitor. But in high school, his mental-ity of "I have to set myself apart from these other people who are growing because that's the only way I'm going to get noticed" kicked in.

He had to stand up for himself a lot. There was teasing like "Hey, munchkin" and "What's up, shorty," stuff like that. Not malicious but enough to remind him, and he wasn't going to put up with it. One time, we were playing Babe Ruth baseball in Palo Alto. He was playing shortstop and I was playing second. Palo Alto had this kid who had definitely hit his growth spurt in middle school; he's like six feet, two hundred pounds. He hit the ball to right and I had my head turned and the kid took this wide turn and plowed me over and started running toward second. The throw came in to Jules and, instead of waiting for the kid, Jules ran at him and jumped on the dude and started trying to punch him. I got off the ground and I was like, "What's going on?!" Jules was yelling, "I got your back, Kurt! I got your back!"

There was one time I definitely got picked on for my size. I was at the skate park at Red Morton when I was fourteen or fifteen. I was out there on my Razor Scooter. (Dad didn't want me on a skateboard. He was afraid I'd break something.) This tall, skinny, eighteen-year-old dude was trying to punk me. I was never scared of anyone. I would talk shit to a big dude even if I knew I was still going to get my ass beat. I got beat up my whole life. So this guy kept at me and I may have said something and he pushed me. I reached up and hit him right in the jaw. He went straight down. I got a little street cred for that one because there were a lot of people there.

There were plenty of fights that didn't go like that, though. I popped off to a teammate once after practice and we were jawing a little. I pushed him and he proceeded to throw my head into the locker and slam it and beat the shit out of me. I was never really afraid to fight. But there was always a strategy. If they are a lot bigger, you have to get that first one in.

Subconsciously, it's all embedded in my head, I guess. When it's "fight or flight," I fight. The way I play, with aggressiveness and attitude, I don't know if it would be the same if

I hadn't been small when I was young. When things happen now in the NFL I don't know if I flash back to childhood, but in the heat of the moment, the reactions I have are the same as they would have been then.

It's a chip on my shoulder, I guess. And I bring it up. Like with Richard Sherman in Super Bowl XLIX against the Seahawks. I get pretty intense during games and was going at him saying, "You're too small! You're too small!" And he said, "You're just a little guy!" I said, "I am, but I'm strong!"

Nicki Edelman

Jules was just tiny. He was going into high school not even five feet, not even one hundred pounds. His skill and talent were outrageous, and I remember him saying, "I could play with these varsity kids but I'm too small." People picked on him a lot. It came out more from kids in high school. It wasn't so much in middle school or elementary because they were all pretty small at that time. He was definitely smaller, but it was a small school that we were at. He had the confidence that scared people off to not mess with him. Once we got into a bigger public school and high school, he was just tiny. I remember him going to Dad at night and saying, "When am I going to grow?" People telling him he wouldn't make it, he wouldn't do anything. In high school, everyone was being recruited to colleges and he wasn't hearing anything. It sucked, he always worked so hard. I just remember a lot of talks with my dad at night saying, "Jules, you're going to catch up. It's going to come. You just got to keep working hard."

Jules is sensitive. Not a lot of people see it. Being small, he never let his guard down, but I've seen it because I'm his little sister. He'll talk to me about how he gets scared sometimes and how he's worried. He talked to me more about stuff as we got older. He would cry. He didn't want to deal with the crap that people were putting him through. He wanted to show everything he had but there was only so much his little body could do and show.

The biggest thing my dad said to us all the time, especially with Julian, was that "Us Edelmans, we catch up. We always catch up. We may not have it at first but we always find a way to do it." Jules lived by that, I lived by that. I still live by that. It takes us longer to get places but we get there. There's no sniveling, no complaining. Just get up, go to work, and get your work done. No one is going to help you, it's all on you.

SIX

WOODSIDE HIGH AND THE MAKING OF A QUARTERBACK

As long as I could remember, I dreamed of going to Saint Francis High School in Mountain View, down the 101 from Redwood City. I wanted to be a Lancer, just like my big brother, Jason. Best football team, best facilities, hottest girls.

Saint Francis's rival was Junipero Serra in San Mateo. That's an all-boys school that, at that time in 2001, had a not-yet-completely-famous alumnus named Tom Brady entering his second season with the Patriots. I wanted no part of Serra. I was born to be a Lancer. Watching Jason play there in front of five to ten thousand people under the lights, my big brother playing cornerback, I saw all I wanted. It was a football and baseball powerhouse in California.

And I didn't get in. I was crushed. This was the first time I had been told, "No. We don't want you."

I was hurt and embarrassed, my tail between my legs. I always talked about going to Saint Francis. After four years of private school at Mount Carmel, I guess I had a little superiority complex, that I wasn't a public school kid. It wasn't grades. I probably had a B average. I wasn't a very good test taker, and I was a little asshole at Mount Carmel. I was Dennis the Menace, and our principal, Theresa Anthony, was not a big fan of mine.

There were things I did at Mount Carmel. For instance, I once took an empty test tube of Raven's Revenge candy (which was basically colored sugar), filled it with colored sand, and sold it to a kid. He chugged it. Got in trouble for that. Another time, I was walking behind a teacher on the playground and did the "suck it" sign (chopping my hands on the tops of my thighs) for a laugh with my friends. A guy across the street saw me and reported me. Across the street! I also got in trouble because my socks were too low, for riding my bike after school without a helmet, and they actually hauled my parents in to talk because I was scoring too many points in basketball. Seriously.

Anyway, I took a tour of Woodside, the local public high school, with Kurt, who was a grade ahead of me. I could tell right away Woodside, with its 1,500 students, wasn't going to be as uptight as the private school I'd been at the previous four years, and that it would be a good fit for me.

The Woodside Wildcats were in the California's Central Coast Section and won back-to-back titles in the Peninsula Athletic League's Bay Division in 1999 and 2000, but there was a new head coach for the program in 2001 named Packy Moss. Dad had stepped down from Pop Warner and was helping out at Woodside. As I started my high school career, he was concerned about my getting smashed. He never had been before.

I was 105 pounds, and unlike in Pop Warner, there were no weight limits in high school. I still had the elusiveness, but when you're barely five feet tall, it's impossible to outrun kids who are almost six feet tall and hitting puberty. I got the shit beaten out of me at running back, ended up hurting my knee and missed six weeks. By the time I came back, the season was dead.

Sophomore year, my running back days were over. We needed a quarterback, and the running back I would have competed with was bigger and faster than me. Dad always wanted me to play quarterback, so naturally he was excited about it. More chances to practice! That summer, we threw every day. I wasn't a natural thrower. Dad was. Our goal was confidence. I had a good arm and I understood the game. I could make good decisions especially on underneath routes. The problem was that it was hard to see—I was practically staring at the center's ass when I came to the line of scrimmage—but I could scramble around and get a sight line and throw deep. We had some very good athletes on that team I could throw it up to.

We were a good team and ended up 9-0 and so did our rivals, Menlo-Atherton. Tradition was that we played each other in the final game of the season. We were playing at their place and it was tied 14–14 with seven seconds left. They had fourth-and-15 at our 43, and I was playing corner for what was going to be the last play. One of their big receivers was lined up on the right and I ran with him. Their quarterback underthrew it and I worked back and picked it off. Game over. Or should have been. Instead of going to the ground, I took a couple of steps trying to return it. That's when I got blindsided by their number 24, who ripped the ball out of my arms and ran it in for the win. Walk-off touchdown. I lost us the game. I was the goat, and not the good kind of GOAT. That day I was the donkey. I was pissed off and upset I let the team down. Overall, though, I was excited about the success I had at quarterback and how the next chapter would go when I went up to varsity.

The summer before junior year, I was working with a quarterback coach named Roger Theder. He had been the head coach at Cal for four seasons in the late '70s, and all the big varsity quarterbacks in the area would go see him. I used to get big-leagued a little bit. I was about five foot five and they were all around six feet, and I can remember Theder shushing me when we'd go for these Saturday-morning sessions. And we were paying for this shit! But I loved to compete against those dudes, so I'd sit there and keep to myself and absorb every single thing he taught.

Realistically, I wasn't the best player but I thought I was. I always had a chip on my shoulder, and now that I was learning drops, throwing techniques, the release area, the route tree, I was feeling like a legit quarterback. One of my receivers, Chris Ruane, would come with me and he'd run routes: the short-out, long-out, slant versus man, slant versus off, skinny post, comeback, play action. It was all footwork and keeping your shoulders open or closed and making sure your balance was perfect. I could do all of that.

After being small for what felt like years, I had a little swagger coming back. We'd gone 9-1 the year before, and the varsity team had been struggling for two seasons under Coach Moss. They went winless in 2001, and 2002 wasn't much better.

I felt like I had a shot at starting. The player I'd be competing with was a senior named Lucas Yancey. That's right, the "Whaboom" guy from *The Bachelorette*. He was our starter. He said "Whaboom!" back in high school. Actually, we all did. You can see us saying it in videos from that season.

I beat Lucas out for the starting spot going into the opener, but in our Wednesday practice that week, I separated my shoulder. I was out for three games until I got a harness made and took a cortisone shot so I could at least come back and play defense. I got some snaps on offense but I couldn't really throw, so I had to run around. Against Aragon High, Lucas separated his shoulder and I was in. I ended up having a pick-6 on defense and forced a fumble that my boy Spencer Garrison scooped up and took to the house. But on offense, I couldn't throw the ball. And honestly, I wasn't that effective running, because I hadn't yet gained size and speed.

At that point, college football wasn't even on my radar. I wasn't looking for the next step. I was just trying to win games and battle Lucas. I was calling my own plays off a wristband, but all I did was throw my favorite routes all the time. I threw verticals because I could hit one of my big guys in the seam. If there were two safeties, I'd have the post receiver down the field or the in-cut receiver underneath. Or I'd hit my shallow crossers or my slant-flats. I learned that from playing *Madden*.

The Aragon game was one of the season's only bright spots. Even though I was playing more at quarterback and had some big games throwing—over three hundred yards against Capuchino—the team was falling apart, a wreck. It was embarrassing.

Guys didn't like Coach. In Pop Warner, Redwood City had the most-disciplined kids. It was like the military. This is high school. It's supposed to be better. It wasn't. It was exactly what I made fun of Woodside for and why I wanted to go to Saint Francis.

In high school, when something was good, we'd say it was "D1," like Division 1, the highest level in college sports. Saint Francis looked D1. We were so not D1. We had no swagger, no attitude. Kids would miss practice, miss lifting. We had talent but we had no direction.

Dad was told earlier that year by Coach Moss that his services were no longer needed. So when he saw how we were struggling, he decided to go see him. I wasn't there, but others told me Dad was pissed off certain kids weren't playing. Finally, Moss said, "Frank, get the fuck out of my office!" My dad said, "Packy, you get the fuck out of my town!"

Dad was told to stay away from the football team for the rest of the season.

On Halloween, it all came to a head. During the day, I did something that stupid high school kids do. I took one of Dad's cars from his shop and went rally racing on some back roads near school. I was going about fifty miles per hour with a car full of guys and doing E-brake slides. It was fun, until I hit a dip in the road . . . and the car stuck. Two tires had popped off the rim, and we were like five miles from school, and we had to get back for a game against Terra Nova. I was petrified that Pops would kill me, but we drove it back all the way to the school on the rims, in time for the game.

We lost to Terra Nova 30–12. It was the fifth loss in a row and we were 2-6, so when the game ended, I didn't even hang around the locker room. I went to the parking lot and sat on the curb wondering what to do, about football and the car.

Meanwhile, in the locker room, someone started a "Fuck Packy!" chant. I don't know who, I don't know how many guys, and I don't know for how long, but when Coach Moss walked in, the chant stopped. He looked around and said, "Thanks guys. Love you, too."

Obviously, it was disrespectful and embarrassing, but guys were fed up. And it shows where we were that year. A bad place. My first year on varsity and this was what it looked like. Our principal made it clear that she wanted the names of the chanters on Monday morning.

When nobody came forward and nobody ratted anyone out, the final two games of our season were canceled. Coach

Moss resigned. The news media descended. There were stories and opinions. As Coach Belichick would say, it was not what we were looking for.

As for the car I ruined? Pops eventually pulled up that night in the blue and white 'Burban and leaned out the window. "What happened to the car?" he asked. "Got a flat," I told him. He could tell I was bummed. He was always a good shoulder to lean on when we lost, believe it or not. He said, "Get in the car." And my junior season of high school was over. Just like that.

I knew the fall of 2004 would potentially be my last season of football. My experience level at quarterback was low. I had a season of freshman-sophomore and a few games of varsity experience. I wasn't polished. College football was by no means guaranteed.

But I knew what I did pretty well, and what needed work. And I was willing to work.

My feet were my best asset. My elusiveness in the pocket and ability to reset and throw were good. My arm was as strong as it had ever been because, after the 2003 football season, I didn't play any other sports as a junior. We wanted my shoulder to fully heal. But I needed to get more accurate and tighten up my motion.

That summer, I worked for Dad at A-1. We got into a nice routine of throwing after work. We'd go to Woodside and Dad would set up bags at different depths for me to hit, all kinds of crazy drills. To this day, I love doing drills, and that's because Dad sold me on drills when I was a kid.

That off-season, I finally started growing. I added about four inches and was five foot nine, 150, when the season started. I still needed to get faster. Dad and I raced one day after a workout. He beat me, looked over, and said, "Yup, still not ready." That was an eye-opener for me. I needed to train, too.

For that, I went to the Riekes Center in Redwood City. I'd been going there since I was about twelve. This place was more than a gym. It was founded by a man named Gary Riekes who played football at Stanford. The aim there was, and still is, to make everyone feel that they are at home when they are there. That they're in a safe place without judgments. There are four divisions of "human enhancement" at Riekes Center: creative arts, athletics, fitness, and nature enhancement. It's a special place, and I owe a lot to Gary for helping me develop in a variety of ways. That summer, I worked even harder.

I also went back to Coach Theder and, after that junior year, I had a little résumé under my belt. Now I was a varsity quarterback, like the other guys had been. I still wasn't his favorite, but he liked me because I did everything he said. For anyone who wasn't my dad, I was extremely coachable. Dad actually was lightening up a little bit, too. He still got on me, don't get me wrong, but it was a little less loud. Maybe I was maturing.

By that time, some of my friends were being recruited and looking at colleges. I took the SATs and I had decent grades, so I was a qualifier, but we made the decision that I'd either go to junior college or go to a prep school. That kind of hurt. I saw all my friends getting their letters to go to different schools, and I hadn't generated any interest. But in California, the junior college route is one a lot of players take. The junior colleges out there are pretty legit in terms of athletics.

I also wanted to make sure our senior football season was a good one. We wanted to prove that the previous year with all the drama wasn't us. We just wanted to play good football and make an impression on anyone at the next level.

Our coach that year was Steve Nicolopoulos. He was a great man and he'd known Dad a long time. It was his second time around as head coach at Woodside, and he'd been through some physical issues in late 1995, when he came down with Guillain-Barré syndrome. It's a nasty disease in which the body's immune system attacks part of the nervous system.

He was paralyzed from the neck down for two months. He had to relearn how to walk and how to feed himself. He coached at Menlo College until 2001 before coming back to Woodside. He was a strong, strong man, and he had a great coaching staff with him. His father, Sam, was on the staff and he made me his special project. He was an older guy by then, but he was always on me for little things like getting out to cover the sideline after I threw to the flat in case I got picked off. The other coaches were Steve Aimnonetti, Larry Howard, Manny Orta, Anthony and Chris Ricciardi, and Larry Schreiber.

After the way things ended my junior year, we needed to do a lot of recruiting to get kids to want to play. We had a beast running back, Tyreece Jacks, and two fast receivers with Andrew Simmons and Spencer Garrison. Our big receiver was Dominic Cruz-Duncan, a guy I could throw it up to. Kenny Walker was a wide receiver and safety. His nickname was "Inka" because he'd chew on pens until they exploded in his mouth. Johnny Anderson was a big athletic tight end who could block and had really good hands.

We had Adam Vukovic at right tackle. Then Sandro Oyola at center. We had a guard named Daniel Sanfelice. Big Coop at left guard—his name was Leonard Ryans, but we called him Coop for some reason. And we had his cousin at left tackle. We had Mike Nizuk, a crazy white kid at fullback. Our middle linebacker was Soni Tuipoloto. Just a missile.

Coach Nicolopoulos

I was aware of Julian before I coached him his senior year at Woodside. When I was at Menlo College in either 1997 or 1998, one of my coaching colleagues brought me this videotape of Julian when he was in Pop Warner. He told me, "You've got to look at this kid. Once this kid grows, he's going to be unstoppable."

There was something about Julian I could see on that tape. You saw the tenacity, the will, the energy, the determination, that he brought to the game. This had to be when he was in sixth grade, God, even before that. It was when he was pretty young. That was the first time that he was brought to my attention.

His size, that was always his shortcoming. All through high school, that was one of the things we had to overcome. But I think he takes the negative things and turns them into positives.

I think the obstacles Frank got through in his life, and Julian's knowing about them, helped him. That gave him the knowledge of how to navigate through his own type of obstacles. They were completely different obstacles, but Julian knew the adversity Frank had grown up with, and that gave him an appreciation for things.

Frank and Angie were always there for Jules, and that is something that a lot of kids don't have. They don't have that father or parents in their corner. Or sometimes they have parents in their corner too much, and Frank could get pretty hard in advocating for Julian or for wanting to see the program run a certain way.

That willingness to say something, to want something to be better, that's not necessarily a bad thing. Julian was a five foot six quarterback for us, but he was so big on the field. He had the attention of all the players. He led by example and he pushed and grinded and beat them up a little bit, but he could get them to go beyond where a normal player would go. He was like a minicoach out there on the field. Julian could back it up. That is one of the great things about Jules as a player, a person, and an individual. He could always back up what he did.

In our game program from that year, I listed my favorite subject as English, my favorite player as Doug Flutie, and my career interest? Lawyer. That year, before the season, I had to be a politician. There were maybe two white guys among the starters. The rest were black guys, Hispanics, Tongans, Samoans; you had to learn a formula for getting guys to work hard. Instead of saying what I said when I was twelve—"Why don't you get your fat ass up and let's fucking go!"—it was more, "Hey bro, wouldn't it be awesome to have a championship? We gotta practice better than this or that's not gonna happen."

We knew we were good, but we weren't sure how good. I had a feeling, though, and one day in the spring while we were running I called over to Coach Aimnonetti and said, "If we go undefeated, Coach, we want a mural right there on the side of the new performing arts building.

He looked at me and deadpanned, "I'll have it done."

Our first game of the season was September 10 against Carlmont High School. We beat them 28–13 and Tyreece had one run in which he lost his helmet and kept going. It was like, "We're heeeerrrreee!"

The next week, we played Gunn, which is a school in Palo Alto. We were down 19–7 with two minutes left when we got a big kickoff return from Johnny Anderson. I had a sixteen-yard reception after I pitched it back to Johnny. On the next play, I hit Spencer for a thirteen-yard touchdown. We forced a Gunn punt, and our guy Paul Tuiono blocked it to give us the ball at the Gunn 23. Soon we were down to our last play. I took the snap and waited for Inka to get open. The corner jammed him at the goal line and I saw I could fit it in between Inka and the right sideline. Inka dove and came up with it as time expired. We won, 21–19.

After that, we knew we couldn't screw around anymore. We didn't. We beat Sequoia, South San Francisco, Mills, Jefferson, Hillsdale, El Camino, and Half Moon Bay by a combined score of 300–89. Tyreece and Spencer were having huge years, and my profile was starting to rise a little because of the way we were all playing.

Then we came to our rival, Menlo-Atherton. The year before, we had to forfeit. This time, our undefeated regular season was on the line. We scored 21 quick ones, then they came back to make it 21–13. In the third quarter, I found Spencer over the middle and he made a one-handed catch and went in for a fifty-two-yard touchdown. But the game actually came down to the last drive before they ran out of time and we won 28–22.

The win made us the top seed in the CCS Medium School division playoffs, where we faced Evergreen Valley in the first round. We smoked them, 56–0. Next we had Terra Nova, the last team we'd played—and lost to—before the previous year had been canceled. We took care of them 39–6.

The championship was played December 3, 2004, in Milpitas, a city north of San Jose. We played Westmont High School, which is 20 miles south of Woodside. By now, I was pretty sure this wasn't going to be my last football game. I'd generated some interest. But we all still wanted to finish the season off the right way. We'd come a long way from where we were on Halloween of 2003.

We had a huge night. I ran for 170 yards and two touchdowns and hooked up with Dominic Cruz-Duncan for a passing touchdown. Tyreece finished off a huge season with a fifty-yard touchdown. He had thirty touchdowns for us that year.

My high school career didn't go at all like I expected it. From not getting in to Saint Francis to being hurt as a freshman and then switching to quarterback because I was too damn small to play running back. Then having our season canceled junior year to a 13-0 season and a championship. For my high school career, I threw for 2,237 yards and 29 touchdowns and ran for 964 yards and 13 more touchdowns. All that in about a season and a half. After all the shit I'd listened to about being too small and all the pounding I'd taken when everyone was growing and I wasn't, I felt pretty good about that.

But what next?

SEVEN

MAKING A NAME AT JUCO

In the first few months of 2005, I was planning my next step. Walk on at UC Davis? Prep school out East? Junior college? I talked about it with my girlfriend, Jaqui Rice. We met in eighth grade when she was at Saint Pius and I was at Mount Carmel. She lived right up the street from us, so I'd ride my bike over to her house after school and we'd go to Taco Bell or shoot hoops in her driveway. I was afraid to go in the house, though, because that would mean running into her dad, who was none other than Jerry Rice. He was a god to me. The first time I saw him, we were shooting hoops and he came out on the front step, no shirt on, all yoked up, gold chain, six-pack abs. I was shook, and I think that might have been the point. Jerry didn't really talk to me and *never* talked to me about football. Even after I made the Patriots and came back after my rookie year to visit Jaqui, he didn't even acknowledge it. Mrs. Rice was always a sweetheart to me.

Jaqui's brother, Jerry Jr., told me that his dad knew who I was. When Jerry Jr. was training to try to make the league, his dad said, "You gotta work like that Edelman kid. He's worked for everything he's got."

I saw Jerry at the Kentucky Derby in 2017. I was with TB and we were all saying hello, and Tom couldn't resist. He said to Jerry, "Hey, I hear Jules spent a lot of time at your house when he was a kid." I don't know if Jerry thought it was funny, but he laughed.

After the season was over, I was still holding out hope of getting into a D1 school, but it wasn't happening at that point. I visited UC Davis, which was 1-AA, and watched a game, but the school didn't give me any paperwork when the visit was over, which pissed me off. The big boy of all the jucos was the City College of San Francisco. That's where you went if you wanted to go D1 afterward. The College of San Mateo (CSM) was up and coming, but at the time, CC of San Fran was the big one. They weren't after me very hard, either.

CSM did show me love. Since I was a qualifier out of high school, I had decent grades and an SAT score that was passable, which meant I could leave after a year for a bigger program. They wanted me as a quarterback.

It wasn't until June that we committed. I was playing in the Lions Bowl All-Star Game at Soquel High, and Larry Owens, the head coach for CSM, was there. Dad saw him standing by a fence. They were old friends. Dad said to Coach Owens point-blank, "Do you really want him?"

Larry said, "Frank, I wouldn't be here if I didn't want him."

The whole process brought me back a little bit to when I didn't get into Saint Francis. It hurt to see all my friends going to four-year universities while I wasn't. This was a crossroads for me. Would I play quarterback? Would they want me to shift to safety? I asked Dad if I should consider switching positions. He said, "You're a quarterback." He was always a confidence builder when I was down.

It turned out that Coach Owens had had his eye on me for about ten years. Frank Guida's son, Bob Guida and Brian

Kelly, who were coaches in Redwood City Pop Warner, told Coach Owens that he needed to keep an eye on me because when I grew, I'd be a pretty good player. In 1998, the year we went to Florida for the Pop Warner National Championship, Coach Owens came and talked to the team and watched practice after. I had no idea who he was, but I guess he liked me even though I weighed only about sixty-five pounds.

Coach Owens also had been at Woodside during his career, so he kept an eye on our 2004 progress and sent two of his assistants, offensive coordinator Bret Pollack and defensive coordinator Tim Tulloch, to scout me in person. They didn't have a problem with a five foot nine quarterback, but I was going to have to earn the job. Which I intended to do. I told the coaches as much during our orientation. They had photos of some of their best players up on the wall, and I said to Coach Pollack, "Where are you gonna put my picture?"

He said, "Yeah, we'll see."

I don't think Coach Pollack loved the comment. We didn't hit it off right away, but Coach Owens loved it because he knew I was coming in to make some noise. If my number one goal was to play quarterback at the Division 1 level, I had to win the starting job in junior college. I went in third on the depth chart behind the returning starter, Kevin Linnell and Jose Avina.

The best thing about the competition was that Coach Pollack used a point system to evaluate everything we did. For example, if you made the right read on a throw, you got a point. If you completed it, you got two points. If you completed it but it wasn't the right read, you got one point. Competition in the late spring was close, so I was always on Coach Pollack during practice about my points. I'd come off the field and say, "Coach, that was nothing less than a 2.8 and if you don't think it is, I'll be in your office tomorrow to discuss it!"

People would ask Coach Pollack why he allowed that. Coach Pollack told them, "He cares. He's competitive. He fights for everything. I'm not going to stop that."

I still drove him a little crazy, because Coach Pollack was pretty competitive himself. Especially when it came to badminton. He ran the program at CSM and knew how to play. I thought I could beat him. So one day in the summer, we started playing. Coach was running me all over the court and beat me 15–1, 15–2. I begged him to keep playing and started to get the hang of it so that the gap was closing. Finally, after about ten games, we stopped. But I had him on the run.

The race to be the starter resumed at training camp. I felt like I was closing the gap, because I was really lighting it up running the ball. Kevin, the returning quarterback, was a good player, too. As the summer wore on, we had a quarterback controversy brewing. I had my guys who'd get loud when I made a play in practice—"That's it, Jules!"—and Kevin had his guys. Since I was the new guy, I knew I had to clearly win. I was doing everything I could to gain people's trust. That meant being a taxi service, too. I had this white S-10 pickup and I'd shuttle my receivers home who didn't have rides. You need to gain that respect.

Right before the first game, Coach Pollack called me into his office and asked if I wanted to "gray shirt," which meant not play in 2005 so that I wouldn't lose a year of eligibility. I could grow, get stronger, and then come back in 2006. CSM would have Kevin as the starter and Jose as the backup.

I wasn't interested. But the competition was so close that Coach Pollack decided we'd split drives in the opening game against Chabot College. Kevin got the first two drives. We scored on the first one and punted on the second. Now it was my turn. First game since high school. First drive. We have a slant-flat combo route. I dropped back . . . pick-6 on my first throw.

I was on the bench like someone had just run over my puppy, wondering if I'd get another opportunity. Kevin took the next two series. I didn't ask if I was going in, I started warming up. Brett came up and said, "You're getting the next drive."

We got out there and had third-and-8 from our 4. I wasn't going to throw unless it was wide open. Nothing came open. So I took off up the middle. I got to the second level and started right, then cut it back around midfield and got to the left sideline and scored a ninety-six-yard touchdown.

We alternated series for the rest of the game and won, 21–14. The next week, we played the College of the Sequoias, and Coach Pollack told me, "We are going to go with Kevin."

I was pissed off. I made some plays, maybe not the right way, but I was making shit happen.

Sequoias was a huge game. They had Brent Schaeffer, a lefty quarterback who "bounced back" from Tennessee (that's the term for someone who comes from a four-year school to a juco). He started the 2004 opener for the Vols as a true freshman but he got into some trouble at Tennessee and landed at Sequoias. He was supposed to be the next Michael Vick. He played like it. Schaeffer got them two quick scores, and Coach Pollack told Kevin he didn't like his body language. It didn't get better so Kevin got pulled. We ended up losing 41–39, but the starter's job was mine from that day forward.

We beat Foothill, 49–0 and I ran for over two hundred yards with three touchdowns. And that's the way the season went along. Big numbers. High scores. It was exciting as hell, and I realized that, knowing how many of these kids were going on to Division 1 or had played at Division 1, I wasn't out of my element at all.

The most important game for me personally was against the City College of San Francisco. I was so wired for that game because I felt I had been an afterthought to them in recruiting. We were 5-2 and the spread offense Coach Pollack had us running was putting up crazy numbers. I had 727 rushing yards and seven touchdowns in seven games, and we'd run for 2,376 as a team. Our offensive line was amazing.

They were 7-0, were one of the best teams in the nation and absolutely never lost to California teams. They had kids like Maurice Purify, a big receiver who went on to Nebraska, and Larry Grant, who ended up at Ohio State. They also had Tyreece Jacks from Woodside.

We punched them in the mouth. First drive, I had a forty-six-yard touchdown run, cutting back on jokers and ducking under dudes. Playing against City, I knew there were scouts there, and it was a performance. You have to have a good game. I did. I scored four touchdowns and ran for 140 yards. But it wasn't good enough, We blew a 24–7 lead and lost 41–40 in the final minute.

CCSF's coach, George Rush, told the media afterward that he was impressed with how I played and said I was "the whole difference" in our team. I was bummed we lost, though, even if I knew I was also performing for colleges.

Larry Owens

I'll never forget as long as I live was when we played the City College of San Francisco. The whole week, it was different for him. He had so much to prove, because he thought they kind of shied away from him in the recruiting process. That week, that day, that game, he put on a show. It was spectacular and I'll never forget it, in part because of the focus he showed. The day of the game, I could hear someone singing, not loudly, but singing a song. I went out and saw Julian, eyes closed with headphones on. He was so ready. I tiptoed back to my office and said, "He is going to take us past them today." We hadn't beaten San Francisco in a long time, so I thought, "Man, this is going to be something different." We didn't win. But it was different. That performance pushed him to be the player of the year in our conference. Everybody got a chance to see what he was really about.

In the final game of the year, we got back at Schaeffer and Sequoias with a last-minute, 41–39 win. We had 528 yards of offense that day. I ran for two touchdowns and threw for two, had 181 yards passing and 145 rushing. For the year, I ran for 1,253 yards and 17 TDs and threw for 1,312 and 14 more scores.

Letters poured in after the season: Florida, Utah, Oregon, Auburn, a bunch of Pac-10 schools, ACC schools, BYU, Boise State. I hadn't been in the recruiting process the year before, so it seemed like a lot. But they all wanted me to stay put, do another year at CSM, and maybe change positions. I wanted to be a quarterback. I knew I didn't fit the mold of the six-five, 220-pound guy with a huge arm. But I knew after that year at CSM I could compete, and I wasn't afraid to say it.

To me, that's important: being willing to say what you plan to do. Mentally, I felt like a gladiator. I vividly remembered that I began focusing on things better at CSM. It was college, so I felt more was at stake. I wanted to win games and really prove to myself and to my teammates that I belonged. You had to face the guys you were going to lead into battle. If you're going out there and demanding hard work from other guys, you have to go out and lead by (a) example and (b) production. That's how you gain respect. I had belief I could do that because I had since Pop Warner.

Now I needed a D1 school.

It wasn't until spring workouts at CSM that I heard something solid. One day, we were walking up this big-ass hill to get to the weight room and Coach Tulloch came up to me and said, "Kent State called and they want to meet with you. They want to give you a ride."

I said, "Who? What is that D2? I told you, Tulloch, I want to go D1."

He said, "No, they're in the Mid-America Conference. The MAC. Teams like Bowling Green, Miami of Ohio. They told me they want to fly you out for a visit."

I was like, "Hell yeah! I'm down."

EIGHT

CHASING JOSH CRIBBS

When I first heard "Kent," I thought it was short for "Kentucky State." I had no idea about the place. All I knew was it was Division 1 and that they were going to let me compete for the quarterback job.

So I took the trip out to Ohio and it was snowing. I'm a California kid. And the campus, it's not Stanford or Cal Berkeley or the beautiful campuses I grew up next to in the Bay Area. The guy who picked me up at the airport and watched over me during my visit was Casey Wolf, who was an assistant in football operations at Kent in 2005 and is still a close friend of mine.

Casey Wolf

My first two years at Kent, our quarterback was Josh Cribbs. By the time Josh graduated in 2004, he'd set every record possible as a dual-threat quarterback. He went on to a ten-year NFL career, including seven in Cleveland, where he was a three-time Pro Bowler as a returner.

After Josh left, our head coach, Doug Martin, decided to go to a pass-based spread offense. He brought in Michael Machen from Coffeyville Community College in Kansas for the 2005 season. Machen had spent three seasons playing minor-league baseball before coming to us, so he was twenty-four years old, and he was big: six six, 230 pounds.

The spread offense didn't work for us at Kent. We went 1–10 in 2005 and 0–8 in the MAC. Coach Martin decided the change was too drastic. He wanted another Josh Cribbs.

In February 2006, a coach named Mark Rhea joined our staff. Coach Rhea was a friend of Larry Owens, Julian's head coach at the College of San Mateo. The consensus out there was that Julian was the best dual-threat quarterback in the state.

Coach Rhea called out to CSM and asked Coach Owens if Julian would make the trip out to Ohio. CSM would have loved to keep Julian for another year, but Coach Owens left it up to Julian. He knew Jules's goal was to get to a Division 1 program.

I spent my first night at Kent in the dorms, hung with some players, and played cards. Finally, I watched practice. I didn't think it was anything crazy good. The juco teams I played against at CSM were really good.

After practice, I sat in a room with Coach Martin. His tactic was to offer a scholarship and get you to commit that day. I told him I wanted to go home and talk to my dad. Coach Martin was a little hesitant. I said, "If I come here, I'm going to start three years. You can wait."

Coach Martin

We really needed two things. We were looking for somebody who could be a playmaker at quarterback, running and throwing. The other thing we needed desperately was—and we honestly didn't know Julian was going to be this until a little bit later—we needed that alpha personality. Kent State was a place that never won. The kids didn't know about winning and neither did the administration. We needed somebody with a personality that could come in there and change the culture of it. We had a kid like that on defense who ended up being Julian's roommate, Brian Lainhart. We felt like if we could get another guy on offense like that, then that would really be something.

When he came on his official visit, he looked me right in the eye and—I will never forget it—said, "Look. I only need to know one thing from you. Am I going to get to compete for the starting job?" I said, "Well, yeah. Absolutely. That's why we are bringing you here, Jules. We need somebody to take control of this team." He said, "Well, then the discussion is over. I'll be your starting quarterback."

He didn't blink. I told our staff, after we signed him, that this kid might be really something special personalitywise. Those guys are hard to find. Julian is one of those rare guys who don't need the players to like them. They are going to respect him because he's going to demand it. He's not worried about being called a coach's boy or being called anything. He's just going to demand that you win and that you go along with him. He was well respected and

had a lot of friends on the team but he rubbed people the wrong way in the beginning because they
weren't used to someone that demanding and that
competitive.

I've always said, Julian has a very healthy chip
on his shoulder. I've been around guys with a chip
on their shoulder who were negative, and they were
a negative to the team. But his was a very healthy
way of looking at things. It spread throughout our
whole football team. He changed the whole football program at Kent State with just his personality.

When I got back to Redwood City, I was on the fence
about Kent. I didn't know what the letters meant, but I was
getting them from Florida, Cal, Utah, from everywhere. And
I was about to commit to little Kent State?

Dad finally said, "Ohio is a cold state. You're going to
learn how to play in the cold. You have nothing left to prove
in junior college. All you can do there is get hurt."

Dad was right. There is a lot of risk going into your second year of juco if you don't put up the same numbers or you
get hurt. You never know, and I'm not like a six-foot-seven
guy that programs will take a chance on if he's hurt. Plus the
fact of having three years to play at D1 instead of two—we
thought about all that and the different scenarios and the
data around it. I decided on Kent State.

All I wanted to do when I got to Kent was win the starting job and win games. I don't know if I was well liked at Kent.
Actually, I know I wasn't. I was an asshole. I was so concerned
about trying to win and compete. I didn't go in there thinking, *Hey, I'm going to be an asshole.* I was simply used to playing on highly competitive teams. We won a championship in

Pop Warner. We went undefeated at Woodside when I was a senior. At CSM, we were a top-10 junior college program. Kent had been a losing environment. The year before I got there, they didn't win a game in the MAC. They won one game all year. I was an intense guy. I didn't go there to lose ten games. I didn't feel like everyone there had that attitude.

I flew into Kent the weekend after my last classes at CSM, got off the plane, and went straight to my first seven-on-seven practice. It was a players-only thing and I had no clue what I was doing with the offense, but I jumped in to take a couple of reps. Practice is the place to earn a little respect. As a quarterback, I'd done the same thing the year prior. You gotta go in and make some noise to get guys to rally behind you. You're not just the starting quarterback, you need to bring leadership and demonstrate that you're a hard worker.

Anyway, I hopped into this drill and threw a skinny post into a post safety, meaning the middle of the field was closed. I thread one in there and I hear a guy in the background say, "You woulda got him killed!" I didn't even know who the guy was and he was talking down on me. It was Machen.

After practice, he was punting some footballs over on the side. I was walking with Brian Lainhart, who was also new there, a true freshman. I walked past Machen and said, "You better keep practicing, because all you're gonna be doing this season is punting the football. You ain't gonna be playing quarterback, that's for sure." I kept walking.

Machen and I didn't get along. There was a bunch of popping off that season. I look back at it now and laugh, but it was tough. The quarterbacks had their clique and did their thing going to country concerts and that sort of thing, and I hung out with the defensive players playing cards.

Coming from the Bay Area, I was used to teams where everyone meshed racially. When I got to Kent, it was more segregated. Not hostile, but people kept to themselves. I was just used to being around Tongans, Samoans, Hispanics, African Americans, dorks, you name it. It was different.

I went and hung out with the defensive backs and guys were like, "What?" I became good friends with Jack Williams, Andre Kirkland, Usama Young, and Brian Lainhart. and we spent time playing cards and *Call of Duty*, or hanging out doing absolutely nothing.

There were times I missed being in California. The way of life, the food, the people. I was from Silicon Valley, where there were surf kids, skater kids, Asian culture, and San Francisco right there being super liberal with hippies, hipsters, 'hood areas, and everything.

When you grow up in California, you hear Spanish every day. In high school or at CSM, Mexican and Hispanic culture is a huge part of your life because you're around it so much. You could get a good-ass burrito and some tacos. I missed that, too. It was meat and potatoes in Ohio. It seemed a little slower. People in Ohio, they love their college sports. The guy works nine to five, has a beautiful little family, cute little house, they get their Friday-night dinner and Saturday they watch their college sports.

Where I'm from, there's a sense of convenience, wherein you have access to pretty much everything. In Ohio, there's not as much, and people are very happy with that. And that was a learning experience for me.

After spring practice, I went back to California and went hard core working out. I went to Riekes a lot, worked with Coach Theder. I was in unbelievable shape and I was nervous. It was my first time leaving California, my first time living on my own. I didn't know what to expect, so I prepared for everything.

Except the humidity. I got to my first practice in Ohio in the heat of summer and, after running like a deer in California, I was like, "Holy shit! I can't breathe!"

In a way, I was happy to be gone from my family a little bit, because I'd been around them for way too long. I would enjoy the freedom, but the little things my parents taught me still stuck. I'd go early to the field and put up those bags for targets like Dad used to do and try to hit them. If I couldn't find a receiver, I'd practice by myself.

I grew up a little. By no means was I mature, but I was in college. I was in a new state, meeting new people, everything was new to me, but it felt normal. Like I was supposed to be there. Mom cried real hard the last time they dropped me off. Jason was out of the house and now I was out of the house and it was just Nicki left at home. And being a teenage boy, I missed Mom, too.

I studied Josh Cribbs. It's who Coach Martin brought me in to play like, and he was a great measuring stick for me. Josh was with the Browns then and was making plays every week. He was the most beloved player on that team. But I wasn't thinking about following Josh to the NFL. I was young and focused on the task at hand. I wanted to win the job and then win football games.

The competition with Machen was a big part of camp. The linemen seemed to pull for him. The receivers were split. The defense sided with me. Guys like Andre, Usama, Jack, Daniel Muir, Gary Ham, those were the guys who swayed the team, and those were the guys I clicked with.

I wasn't able to showcase what I could do until we went live in practice with full tackling. In a red jersey, a guy could tag me and I'd be down. I felt like, *If I didn't have the noncontact jersey on, I'd have scored.* Once the pads went on, that's when I won the job. I was making guys miss all over the place and Coach Martin said that was the difference maker. I was still growing, too, and getting faster. I didn't have long speed, but I had short speed. Once I saw I could make guys miss at this level, I knew I had the answers.

When Coach Martin went with me, he said, "This is your team." Obviously, Machen wasn't happy with it by any means. But I wasn't worried about other people's feelings. I was more concerned with learning the system and trying to win college football games. That rubbed people the wrong way a lot of the time. I didn't click with some guys on the team, because I didn't totally respect them. I didn't think they did everything they possibly could for the team. It was one of those things where I might have come off like an asshole but I didn't care. I was out there trying to win games. If you hate me, you hate me. But I know you're going to respect me because I'm gonna lay it on the line and give literally everything I have on the field, even if it's not what's best for me or if I should be preserving myself. I didn't care. I had the "let's make a play" mentality. I didn't just dip my toe in. That's not how I was brought up. If you're gonna compete, you're gonna compete. I was never uncomfortable competing. Of course there's pressure and butterflies, but that's okay.

Coach Martin

Julian was a unifier. You can't fake that. You can't fake being able to get along with different types of people, and Jules had that. He fit in with everybody. Anybody who wanted to have that same mentality, you were welcomed in his circle. There were a lot of guys who, because they had been used to losing for so long, didn't want to hang out with him early on. Then as guys got to know him better and knew what he was all about, all of a sudden everybody started gravitating to him. He was really popular with our team before long.

My first college game was August 31, 2006, at Dix Stadium in Kent, Ohio. We got blown out by Minnesota, 44–0. It was kind of expected but I was bummed. Three interceptions in my first start. The next week, we played Army at West Point. I threw my first touchdown pass to my buddy Najah Pruden, who was a senior wide receiver and one of the team's real leaders. The pass was a duck but Najah went up and got it. We lost in double overtime, 17–14, but we came out of that game with a lot of confidence. I felt like we were all starting to come together a little.

The next week, we played at Miami of Ohio. Hadn't won there since 1972, but we beat them 16–14. That started a five-game winning streak, the first since 1977. We beat the brakes off Bowling Green, then we had Akron, our rival game.

That's all I had to be told. I didn't know Akron but I figured they were the same as the Sunnyvale Black Knights in Pop Warner or Menlo-Atherton when I was at Woodside. Akron was close by, they had better facilities than us, and they had a stud quarterback named Luke Getsy. Anytime there was a stud quarterback on the other side, I took that as a challenge and wanted to outplay him and say, "I'm five ten, bro, what's up?" Class attendance was optional for me that week. All my focus was football and holding the Wagon Wheel, which was awarded to the winning team. We won 37–15 and I had my best all-around game: 17 for 21, for 305 yards and two touchdowns, and 24 carries for 69 yards and another touchdown.

After a win at Temple, we were on to Toledo. And I took this one personally. Coach Rhea, who'd recruited me, left Kent for Toledo right after I committed. I wanted to create some hatred and I directed it at him. I was almost too geared up for that game, and I had a lot to say. A big defensive end lit me up from behind and I was hurting. I got up in his face and said, "That's all you fucking got, bro!? You're fucking soft!" I'm the quarterback doing that. So stupid.

I had a long run near the Toledo sideline and saw Coach Rhea and said, "You left us, huh!?" I just wanted to rip his head off. I don't know why. I felt he was very disloyal to me and that he felt too good to be where I was at. I don't have hard feelings now, of course, but in the heat of a game I like to have a cause to play for sometimes. Another time I saw their head coach, Tom Amstutz. He passed me over because I wasn't big enough. I yelled to him, "Am I too short now?!" A little bit obnoxious, I know.

But we were on a five-game streak and the enthusiasm was flowing. We were playing Ohio University and the winner would sew up the MAC East and get a bowl game. That didn't happen at Kent. Unfortunately, it didn't happen in 2006, either. The weather went through all four seasons that day: it started off warm and muggy, two storm fronts came through, there was rain, there was snow, there was a forty-minute lightning delay and thirty-three m.p.h. winds. And we had two punts in the first half that traveled a total of six yards. The first actually lost a yard. Ohio scored on both drives after the bad punts. And that was pretty much it.

Their coach, Frank Solich, was such a brilliant coach. He'd been at Nebraska before that and his team was disciplined. I ran for 121 yards and threw a touchdown, but I wasn't that great, either. I was so pissed. After the game, Coach Solich shook my hand and told me what a great game

I had. Being the young punk I was, I said "Coach, you better not lose another game because we're right on your back."

I'm a poor loser. I don't know whether I enjoy winning as much as I hate losing. Even when you win, you start looking around for the next thing. There's satisfaction, but it's temporary. You don't even really enjoy it. It's cool, you hit your pinnacle, but what's next?

Coach Martin

Frank [Solich] loved Julian. Frank actually came up to me at one of the coaches' meetings after that season and said, "You know what Edelman said to me after the game?" I said, "I don't know if I want to know." He said, "He came right up to me, shook my hand, got right in my face and said, 'You better not lose one game or I'll catch you in this league.'"

I think things would have been a lot different for Kent State if we'd won that game. We would have had a bowl game, which would have gained the program more money and exposure. That would have helped with facilities, all of which would have helped with recruiting. It's hard at smaller Division 1 programs to get the traction you need to change the culture. We almost did, but that game really hurt the process.

The season went downhill after that. I got hit from the blind side the next week against Buffalo and a 14–0 lead wound up being a 41–14 loss. I separated my sternoclavicular joint (SC joint for short), located where the clavicle meets the sternum at the base of the neck. I couldn't take a breath.

Next up was Virginia Tech. They were twentieth in the nation and I really wanted to play against Michael Vick's school even if he wasn't there anymore. But Coach decided not to play me because he wanted me to get healthy for the MAC games left. We wound up getting shut out there, 23–0. To give you an idea of how young I looked still, ESPN televised the game and in the fourth quarter, they were talking about Coach Martin's high school–aged son who was playing baseball. They thought I was Coach Martin's kid and put the camera on me the whole time.

We beat Eastern Michigan 14–6, but my shoulder was a mess and I knew I couldn't make all the throws. I was in a funk. I just didn't feel right and we got out of there with a win but I knew I held us back.

Then we went into Ball State and our coach had a bowl game lined up for us if we won. We underestimated them. We went into Muncie, Indiana, and got our asses kicked, 30–6. It sucked. We were 5-2 at one point, we could have been 6-1, and then to finish 6-6? It was terrible.

Some guys were content with that season because we'd had the most wins we'd had in a long time and were bowl eligible for the first time in years. Just a lot of bullshit stats.

I had a surgery on my labrum so I was in Kent rehabbing that thing the whole year. That was long. I didn't get to do the off-season training, which meant I couldn't train hard, so I wasn't getting any better. And that's what the off-season is for: improving yourself, ultimately. You find the things you didn't do well and work on them and polish the things you did do well. And there was none of that, because I wasn't throwing for four months.

That was the first time I had to deal with a big injury. My arm got really weak and of course I pushed it too far trying to come back. I learned a lesson. Psychologically, coming back from injury ruins me, because I can't work the way I want to work. I feel like I'm losing ground on people. They're making gains and I'm just trying to get back to where I was.

We opened up in 2007 with a win at Iowa State. My arm strength still wasn't there but I was getting more fast and explosive. Kentucky was next, Coach Martin's alma mater. We were looking forward to a good showing there against a team that had Andre Woodson at quarterback and Stevie Johnson at wide receiver. I was playing well athletically but not great schematically, and I was responsible for two turnovers in the first half. We were still tied 14–14 at the break but I dinged up my knee and couldn't change direction. I wound up with 135 yards on the ground but I was pissed off about losing. Coach Martin said after the game that the fans in Kentucky gathered at our tunnel to applaud me and the running back Eugene Jarvis, but I didn't even hear them. Our momentum from the previous year's winning streak seemed so far away. Besides that, now I had the knee.

We beat Delaware State but I tried to run only four times all game and it was driving me crazy because I just couldn't cut. We figured it was just a sprained knee, and I had a knee sleeve put on it. That didn't do shit to help me. Akron was next, and we were again playing for the Wagon Wheel. During one long run, I remember yelling over to our team doctor, who was a great guy, "Doc! I can't! Fucking! Cut!" We ended up losing 27–20, and I did not play well.

We beat Ohio 33–25. We played a fundamentally good game, and we really didn't do that too often. I was a big offender when it came to that. Whenever we lost, I was turning the ball over. If I could take back one thing, it would be how reckless I was with it. I'd be hurdling guys, carrying the ball like a loaf of bread. Just unprofessional. We also lost games on special teams. It wasn't just momentum shifts in the kicking game. It was plays that led straight to losses. Fundamentally, we could be terrible, but we were dangerous. We had enough athletes that we could mess a team up if we got hot.

We lost to Miami (OH) 20–13. Again, we could have beaten them, but I had two interceptions and the season was starting to go to shit. The next week, we were at Ohio State. Every kid in Ohio loved that school, but I didn't know the aura around it. I was a California kid; I didn't know college football was a complete way of life out there. People loved their Stanford games, but the Bay Area was a pro area. I loved the Niners. Other guys loved the Raiders. You'd root for college teams but you didn't follow them, you weren't fanatical. And that's what it is in Ohio. It's unreal to see it. Ohio State everything. Kids would leave Kent games to go watch Ohio State games, and that pissed me off. I wanted to play in that setting against a team that good, but I got only a couple of series before they shut me down for the day to save me for the rest of the MAC games.

As it turned out, my season ended against Bowling Green. By that time, we were losing, and I was starting to take off running at crazy times. On one play in the second half, I was just going into a slide when I put my arm down and a guy dove into it. I wasn't 100 percent at the time, and the teams I torched the year before, when I was 100 percent? They wanted a piece of me. At least that's how I felt. We'd embarrassed some teams the year before. This time around, they were trying to hit us and hurt us.

My hand was planted on the ground and it just wiped out my arm. It wasn't a pop, it was a tingle. I looked down and there was a bump sticking out that looked like a golf ball in my arm. I'd had those before on my hand or forearm where it flares up and usually it was just a pocket of blood that looked ridiculous.

I got up and slapped it and it was sore. So I said, "Aw fuck, I don't know if I can do this." In the huddle I started moving my wrist and I saw the lump sliding up and down. So I said, "Coach, I think I broke my arm." He said, "What?" I said, "I think I broke my arm!" He went, "Are you hurt?" I said, "Yeah!" He went, "Well, get down." It was broken. I snapped my radius. I had a plate and eight screws thrown in there.

Now I was rehabbing again for something stupid. I was going down that rehab road again. Meanwhile, that was it for my season. A freshman, Giorgio Morgan, came in to replace me. He threw for 247 yards and three touchdowns in his first game before getting hurt the next week against Northern Illinois. But he played well. Well enough to start talk that I might get moved to wide receiver my senior year.

Giorgio was a strong-armed guy, big and mobile. But I felt disrespected that people even thought there should be a competition. I thought we'd done good things in my time starting. On the other hand, I look at it in hindsight and I can see that I was a crazy-ass player. I turned it over. I had to play well for us to win, and sometimes I might have tried to do too much.

That off-season, once my arm was healed and I started training, I felt that pressure. I started to feel the fear of, "Is this my last year of football? What am I gonna do?" I had to go in and once again get back on the grind because I felt the insecurity of people thinking I shouldn't be the guy.

I created more options for myself that off-season. I started doing more Olympic lifting, which I'd never done as a quarterback. I'd do leg press, dumbbell bench, but really nothing else. So I took some pride in the whole training process. We hired this guy Tobias Jacobi, who was a tough-ass dude. I developed a relationship with him and he worked me hard. I could tell I was getting stronger when we ran the bleachers. Before, I'd struggled a little. By that off-season, I could beast it. I was a raw athlete after my first year. After my second year I had the injuries. My third year I put my heart into training.

I also had to consider what would happen if football was over for me after the upcoming season. That summer, I stayed in Kent with Brian Lainhart and Cobrani Mixon, two of my good friends. Brian and I went back to his hometown in Cincinnati, and he put me in touch with some of the firehouses down there to line up a job. You never know. My dad always said that a fireman can work three days and have four days off, so he can have another job. And there's team camaraderie in a fire station. It's like a locker room. I knew I needed to keep my options open.

Brian Lainhart

That whole off-season, people felt there was something brewing. The way Giorgio played after Julian got hurt, people thought Giorgio would be the starter. So when Julian was motivating people and it was rubbing them the wrong way, they weren't responding, as if to say, "Why is the backup telling me to work harder?" It was one thing when we were rolling, but now people were looking at him and are thinking, "Our quarterback is Giorgio Morgan."

I got in a lot of altercations because of Julian, because I wasn't going to see him disrespected. I'll never forget sitting in the academic resource center when one of our wide receivers who thought he was good but never played walked up and said something smart to Julian, something along the lines of him not being any good. Julian said to him, "Don't worry about me." Then here came Giorgio, and the receiver said to Julian, "You should worry about him

[Giorgio] because he just took your job and he's our quarterback."

Once spring ball came around and Julian was healthy, it wasn't any competition. I knew Coach Martin knew that, too. But in the second game of the year against Iowa State, Julian had a rough game. He threw three touchdown passes but he had a couple of turnovers, one deep in Iowa State territory. We lost 48–28, and I knew he was crushed. He was so bent on proving to everyone that he was the guy, and he had that type of game you'll have when you try too hard.

People were wondering, "Are we going to see Giorgio?" Julian was upset that night. He had tears. His parents, even Coach Martin were concerned. It was a hard time, mentally. A low point. But a couple of weeks later, against Ball State, he got his swagger back. He was a one-man show offensively. The way he carried himself, and the way he produced and the way he made things happen, was just Julian being Julian.

The game was basically over late and Julian was still out there flipping over people and landing on his head. Most guys would have slid. Not Julian.

We opened my final season at Boston College. That defense was stacked. I was kind of nervous because I hadn't played in a live game in a while and been in a red jersey for all of camp. Whenever I come back from an injury, I just don't know how it will react or if I'll feel the same. BC threw us around and I threw a red-zone pick to Mark Herzlich, but the game was competitive and it was a good measuring stick for where we were. I picked up confidence as the game went on, thinking less about the injury and realizing how much the off-season lifting program had worked.

But I was not good in that loss to Iowa State. It was hard knowing that my mistakes were costing us. We were a better team than we were showing, and I was a better player. I was pretty low at that point.

After an easy win over Delaware State, we lost two in a row on the road at Louisiana Lafayette and Ball State. Against Louisiana Lafayette, I had 136 yards, my highest rushing output so far. We weren't winning, but at that point, I felt I was running better than I ever had.

Down the stretch of my senior season, we leaned on that. Before that season, I'd had two games over one hundred yards rushing. I was over a hundred in eight of our final nine games. In addition to that, Coach Martin started using me on special teams.

Against Akron—a heartbreaking loss in double overtime—I was the punt protector on snaps. Coach felt the threat of a short snap to me kept the return team honest and helped our coverage unit. Coach also put me back a few times at the end of the season to field punts. He did it mostly to show NFL scouts that I had punt-return skills. It had worked for Josh Cribbs. Unfortunately, I was pretty raw and didn't break any, but at least it gave me some advance preparation just in case.

One of the hardest things about that last year was that we never got back to where we were in 2006 when we won five straight. As guys from that year graduated and moved on, the losing culture just seeped back in, like there was a sense of futility in trying too hard.

There were times I lost it because of that. One of the times came during a practice my senior year. We were working on bubble screens, and I threw it behind one of our receivers,

Sam Kirkland. He didn't even try for it, he just kind of turned his head and let it fall. I told him not to do it again. The next rep, he did it again, so I chased him down and we got after it a little. Coach Martin let it go for a second, then blew the whistle and started yelling for us to break it up. Coach was a different cat. He got fired up when I got fired up. If it got me playing well, it was good by him. He took a lot of heat for some of the shit I did on the field, like turning the ball over and making crazy plays, but he stood by me.

Coach Martin

Yeah, that fight happened. You could see it coming. He's right, we had the bubble drill going and the guy didn't make a good effort and Julian warned him. He said, "I'm just telling you, one more time and I'm coming after you." Sure enough, one more time happened and Julian got after him. I will say this, that kid changed, Sam Kirkland. That kid ended up being a really good player and a really good friend with Julian. It really turned his career around. Julian held everybody to a high standard. All the other players had to come to his standard; he wasn't going to come back down to theirs. That's why Kent State had been a losing program for so long. Everybody was willing to accept the status quo—and he wasn't. He raised everybody up to his level, and I knew that was happening. You could see it happening with our football team. I talk to players all the time about not being worried about being a coach's boy. You guys have to want to win more than I do. He was one of those guys.

When it came time to play Bowling Green, I decided to generate some hate. This was the team that had broken my arm the year before. Now we were back at it. With a Sharpie, I circled the still-red scar on the inside of my forearm just to remind me that they were the villain and I wanted revenge.

It didn't really work. We lost 45–30, but I had 170 on the ground with two touchdowns. I also threw a pair of interceptions.

The last game of the year was Buffalo. I did not want to end my college football career with a loss, but it was a close game. We were up 24–21 and running our clock-killing offense. We needed a first down to bleed the clock and end the game. With 1:46 left, we took over after an interception. Pretty soon, it was third-and-11. Buffalo called a time-out. Coach Martin called a read option. If we picked up a first down, the game was ours. I went around the right end with the ball and had some room on the sideline, but just before the sticks I was met by three Buffalo defenders. I couldn't go around them, so I tried to go through them. I put my head down and bulled forward. We needed eleven, I got twelve. We won, 24–21.

But I was sad. It was my last game at Kent. That school—and Coach Martin—had taken a chance on me. I developed a special relationship with Coach Martin and appreciated everything he'd done for me.

After the game was over, I didn't know what was next. I didn't know where I was going. Or if I was going anywhere at all.

NINE

SO YOU THINK YOU'RE A WIDEOUT

Canada seemed the likeliest destination for me to play pro football. Canadian Football League (CFL) scouts checked me out at Kent, and I was still committed to playing quarterback. The CFL, with its wider field, was a nice fit for a dual-threat guy like me.

It made sense. After all, I grew up idolizing Doug Flutie and patterned some of my game after him. There was no better CFL quarterback than Doug, so maybe it was the best fit for me. As a senior, I ran for 1,370 yards, threw for 1,820, and I was still getting better at the position.

It's not like the NFL would be crying if I went to Canada. I wasn't even invited to the Combine in February 2009, where all the best prospects were evaluated by NFL teams. I knew I wasn't going to play quarterback in the NFL at 5-10. I'd have to convert to wide receiver—which I'd never played— or become a kick-return specialist (which I'd also never done except for my awkward returns in my last game at Kent). Josh

Cribbs had made the conversion, but would I get the same chance? Making it to the NFL was going to be an uphill climb.

Meanwhile, the CFL's British Columbia Lions claimed my negotiating rights. Their player personnel director, Bob O'Billovich, thought I had a lot of promise.

That kind of situation meant I needed some representation and advice, but the agents that approached me at Kent didn't impress me. Finally, Coach Martin stepped in and recommended me to his agent, Don Yee, at Yee and Dubin Sports in Los Angeles.

Coach sent Don a highlight film, and we heard back quickly. Don said, "We want to fly you out to LA. We want to meet with you." I was like, "Hell yeah! It was LA, a big-time agent. When I found out they represented Tom Brady, I thought, "Holy shit!"

When I got to LA, I sat down with Don and Carter Chow. Carter was new at the time but is now still my agent and one of my closest advisers. Don asked me, "What do you want to do?" I told them I wasn't sure. The NFL was my ultimate goal, but I didn't know if it was realistic.

Don said, "Well, after watching your film, I want to call you 'Dizzy,' you make defenders spin so much. I personally think if you go to the NFL in the late rounds or even undrafted, it's gonna be hard for a team to cut you."

Carter Chow

There was an offensive lineman at Kent State who scouts were talking about in 2008, but watching his film, Don and I just kept seeing this little quarterback running around making play after play after play.

Don said, "Never mind the offensive lineman, I want the quarterback." We offered to bring Julian down to our office after the season. He walked in wearing baggy jeans, an oversize white T-shirt and white Air Force 1s. He had a shaved head and two diamond studs. He looked the furthest thing from an NFL player with that baby face.

But he was super, super intense. The guy had been told "you are too small" so many times in his life and had overcome all of that and accomplished what he had accomplished at that point because of his intensity. We talked for a couple of hours and then, as we got ready to take him back to the airport, he asked to use the restroom.

He went to the bathroom, came out, and said, "Carter, I want to sign with you." I said, "Right now?"

He said, "Yeah, let's do it right now." He had called Frank from the bathroom and they had talked about it and made their decision.

We told him, "Hey, you're not going to be a quarterback in the league. Maybe you can be a running back, maybe a special teams guy, but what do you think about receiver?" He said, "Well, I've never caught a ball before, but I'll figure it out."

That "I'll do whatever I can to stay on the team and get out on the field" attitude is what has always driven Julian.

The CFL was plan B, but we felt like he was an NFL player. What he showed athletically could translate to the NFL. For us, it was all about finding the right team, scheme, position, and situation where he would have the best chance to succeed. We immediately went to work trying to figure out how we could best accomplish that. The skill set was there, it was just the matter of finding the right spot for him.

At that time, the league was trending toward a smaller scatback type of player who could catch the ball out of the backfield. The Wildcat was getting popular at the time as well, and we knew Julian could do some of that.

We hoped that he could catch the ball, but I don't think any of us thought he would become the number one wide receiver he's become. Talking to teams in the lead-up to the draft, we said, "Hey, look, he may not have played the position before, but if you give him a chance and the opportunity, this is what we think he can do for you." It was going to be a little bit of a leap of faith for whatever team ended up taking him.

Coach Martin had said the same thing Don did: I would be hard to cut. They both believed I could be a returner and special teams guy. And a slot receiver. Like Wes Welker. But the BC Lions made their offer. It was an incentive-based deal that had a base of about $60,000 and a maximum value over $150,000.

Take that, or take a shot at chasing the NFL dream?

I thought, "*A hundred grand*! Hell yeah, that's a lot of money!" So I said, "What do you think, Don?"

Don said, "I think you can play in the NFL."

Well, I didn't grow up dreaming of playing in Canada. And that's when I made the decision that it was time to change positions. Which started me on a grueling path to the NFL draft.

I went home to work out with Dad and we'd go run the Jerry Rice Hill that he supposedly ran at Cañada College.

When I finished one day, Dad asked, "Did you beat those five guys?"

"What five guys?" I said.

"The five kids that are working right now to beat you out of what you are trying to accomplish."

Since I wasn't invited to the Combine, I had to make a big impression at Kent's pro day. Teams from around the NFL sent scouts, coaches, and personnel men to the one-day workout where we'd be tested for strength, speed, smarts, you name it.

Don asked if I wanted to train in Los Angeles or Cleveland. I was still taking night classes so I decided I'd train in Cleveland at Speed Strength Systems in Euclid. Tim Robertson was the owner and was known for being a Combine training guru. He's still going strong training athletes, including last year's number one pick in the NBA draft, Ben Simmons, and dozens of other NFL players.

It was like *Rocky IV* when he was training in Russia. I'd get up at 5:45 and drive fifty-five minutes in a pickup truck with no heat to get to a huge tin building that felt like an old factory. This was a big deal. I was nervous about testing because I was always a quarterback, and quarterbacks get special treatment. You don't have to do all the testing everyone else does, you just dick around throwing footballs at the goalposts until they're done.

One important thing I learned was nutrition. I didn't know how to eat, so I would just eat off the dollar menu at Burger King or McDonald's like a poor college kid. It made me change my routine. In the morning I had to eat two cups of oatmeal, four eggs, and two pieces of toast, then drink thirty-two ounces of water and sixteen ounces of orange juice. No butter. I used fat-free Pam. Everything was super clean. I'd cook up four egg whites and one egg yolk because I liked the taste of the yolk. I would cut up some deli turkey and that was my breakfast.

I went out to Walmart and would buy everything in bulk, things like sixty four-ounce pieces of tilapia. Cheap as hell, but it's a really healthy meal and clean, nothing really in it. I would have a four-ounce tilapia with a cup and a half of brown rice. Then I would have two cups of frozen broccoli and thirty-two ounces of water. At lunch, I would come home and make healthy sandwiches. If we went to Subway, I would eat a clean turkey sandwich with no mayo, no nothing, and an apple. I didn't eat anything bad, literally. I didn't eat real sugar for about three months.

Within four weeks, I could definitely see the results. Working out six days a week, eating five meals a day, drinking protein between meals, I was losing weight down to 190 but I was stronger and more defined. It was cool to see results, but when you stay disciplined, you sacrifice fun. My cheat days would be having a salad at Ruby Tuesday with some ranch dressing on it.

I had a phobia about being late or underprepared, so I'd be in bed by 9:00 p.m. My routine: Up at 5:00 a.m., eat breakfast and leave at 5:45. Work out at Speed and Strength from 6:30 to 11:00. Then I'd go back to Kent and have someone punt to me. At night, before I went to class, I'd go to the indoor track facility and catch about four hundred balls. Why? Because I was so far behind. Dad kept telling me, "You're ten thousand balls behind these guys because you haven't caught balls for four years. These guys you're competing against are like little fine-tuned machines, all coming from four-year programs."

I was miles behind. How could I impress NFL scouts as a receiver if I barely knew how to run routes? Enter Charlie

Frye. Charlie was an Ohio kid who went to Akron. He spent two years with the Browns and two in Seattle. Now he was a free agent trying to stay sharp and get another contract.

He was a longtime client of Tim Robertson's. One day, he came up to me and said, "I want you to run routes with me. I'll teach you." I don't know why he offered, but we worked out at the indoor facility at Akron. Charlie was a stud, just a cool guy. I was in awe of him.

Charlie Frye

Why did I help Julian? Because I never saw someone more dedicated to making it. From the minute I met him, every decision I saw him make—literally—was about getting himself closer to ultimately getting drafted.

By that time, I'd been in the NFL a few years, but I went to Akron. I knew the road he had ahead of him. Before I started working with him, I asked the head coach at Akron at the time, J. D. Brookhart, "Can this kid play?" JD said, "Absolutely." And he'd coached Larry Fitzgerald and Antonio Bryant at the University of Pittsburgh.

Not only was he electric in the way he moved but his work ethic was second to nobody I'd ever seen. I played for the Browns with Josh Cribbs, who busted his ass and was a terrific playmaker. Julian worked on another level. You would have to kill him to stop him from accomplishing his dream. I thought I worked hard? Julian wore me out.

The kid was over the top with his commitment. After we threw, I would take him to Subway right across from the indoor facility. He would order the turkey sandwich and get every vegetable they had. I said, "Man, put some damn mayonnaise on that! Nobody wants to eat a dry sandwich." He wouldn't put one squirt of mayo on there because he knew it was bad for him.

When it came time for his workouts, I wanted to be there for him. NFL scouts and coaches would come in and see me and say, "What the heck are you doing here, Frye?" I would say, "This is my guy right here, man."

The Patriots came in the most. Last time they were there, they said, "Don't you tell anyone about this kid."

I told them I'd already called my owner out in Oakland, Mr. [Al] Davis. Too bad for Oakland, though. They thought he was too small and too slow.

Charlie taught me some of the basics: How to cut sharply and not roll the route. That was one thing I could do. Even though I was inexperienced as a wideout, my lateral quickness and cutting ability was better than the guys I was training with. Getting open isn't all speed. It's precision and creating separation, and when you're quick, you can open up space with one step.

My daily routine evolved into leaving Speed Strength at 11:00 a.m., slamming a protein shake and Charlie taking me and maybe another two guys to Subway. He'd buy us sandwiches and bust my balls because of the way I ordered it. "Bro, no chips? No mayo?" I always had the apples and never got the cookie. Then we'd drive forty-five minutes to Akron and run routes. We did that four days a week. Some guys would cancel, but I went every time. I had tunnel vision. After training with Charlie, I'd get back to Kent around 4:00 p.m., eat a handful of nuts and take a nap. Class would be from 5:30 to 8:30 p.m. Then I went home, ate dinner, went to bed, and started again the next morning. I could have stopped going to classes but at the time, I was going to be the first Edelman to graduate (my sister, Nicki, beat me to it). It was important to Mom and Dad and it's still important to me. I only have two classes left to take but I need to hunker down and finish.

Inevitably, there had to be some drama to my training, and it came two weeks before pro day. I broke my jaw in a fight.

During training, things get competitive with the other guys. If we raced and I won, I would let you know. It was the nature of the beast. But there was a receiver from Akron in the group and we didn't like each other. One day, we exchanged words. He pushed me. I pushed him. He popped me in the face. I tackled him and we were rolling around on the ground until it got broken up. When I got up, it felt like I'd broken a tooth in the back. It just felt loose.

It wasn't a tooth. Broken jaw. I had to call up Don Yee and Carter Chow and tell them. They were not happy. They told me, "This is not going to look good when an NFL scout sees you with a wired jaw." My mouth had to be wired shut and I had to wear a stupid headgear thing. I was scared about how much weight I'd lose so I was drinking five-thousand-calorie shakes throughout the day. When pro day came, I went to the dentist and had him unwire me so I could open my mouth and make it seem like the rest of the appliance was just braces if a scout asked. I also took off the headgear.

I couldn't really talk, though, so I sounded like I had rocks in my mouth. Not the best impression. But I made up for it when I tested. We drew a lot of teams that day thanks to our left tackle, Augustus Parrish. He was a big boy who teams wanted a look at, so we had the 49ers, Packers, Dolphins, and a few others. It wasn't like Ohio State's pro day, but it was a good turnout.

We had a weigh-in (I was 196 after I chugged three bottles of water) and then did the bench press with 225 pounds. I was so scared because I wanted to do at least fifteen reps but I knew there was a chance I might not get to double digits. I just didn't work out for that as a quarterback. I hit fourteen and that took some stress off.

Then we ran the 40. I wanted to get in the 4.4s but they had me at 4.51. Then they stuck the Wonderlic intelligence test in there, which I thought was ridiculous because you're in the middle of a workout and here comes this test when you're all anxious. After the Wonderlic, we were back to drills. I ran the three-cone pretty well. That tests change of direction, and it's all about sticking the turns.

Next came the short shuttle, also known as the 5-10-5, which tests lateral quickness, explosion, and speed. Two cones are set up ten yards apart and there's one cone in the middle. You start at the middle cone, explode to your left five yards to reach the first cone, sprint ten yards back to the opposite cone, then return five yards to the cone in the middle. Four seconds is a great time.

There were about a dozen guys in our group and I hit it pretty well when it was my turn. When everyone else had gone, the scouts made me run it again. I had a couple of buddies standing there yelling, "Yo, you ran a 3.99. They don't believe it!"

I ran it again and I timed even better: a 3.91. That time would have been the best at the Combine. If I'd been invited. I also killed it in the long shuttle (60 yards) with a 10.74. That also would have been the fastest at the Combine.

We followed up the drills with some routes. Charlie actually came and threw for me. He was really looking out for me and we had our timing down by then. He also knew all the routes they'd want to see so I was so well prepared. After that, I fielded some punts and kickoffs and the Steelers had me do some defensive back drills.

After the workout, one of the scouts wanted to spend a little more time talking so he took me to lunch. So now I had to eat with a broken jaw and I could barely talk. I was over there eating a tuna sandwich, licking the fish out and swallowing it whole. Great look.

With pro day over, Don and Carter started getting calls. I worked out at Kent for Miami, Chicago, Green Bay, and Cleveland. I was so appreciative of every team that came to see me. And I was grateful to the people who trained me: Tim and Charlie. I realized then that training is the edge you can get on guys. If you're eating clean, doing everything you can, and not partying, you can make gains. At that point, I had the motivation of thinking about having to work at the shop with Dad. That was in the back of my mind the whole time: "What am I going to do after this?"

Miami flew me down for a visit. Tony Sparano was the head coach and Jeff Ireland was the GM. I dressed in a nice suit, was very quiet and respectful. Don and Carter kept reminding me, "It's a job interview. Everything you do and say counts." I was definitely a little nervous, and the teams like to see you nervous to see how you deal with stress. In Miami, they asked me about a citation I got at Kent for having an open container of alcohol. There were two houses side by side where there was a party and I walked on the sidewalk to go from one to the other. When I did, a cop popped out of a van parked on the street and he cited me. I was pretty surprised they had that on me.

In Chicago, I met with the coaches and the GM, Jerry Angelo. I really felt like I was presenting well at these meetings because I knew football. I could get up and explain concepts and schemes and go over my protections. I could really break it down. Then Jerry said to me something like, "You played quarterback in the MAC. You're a running guy. You've never played wide receiver. You have subpar talent there. We are probably not going to draft you. We are thinking more of you as a priority undrafted free agent to claim after the draft."

I was so pissed about that, just the simple fact that he wasn't going to draft me. I didn't tell him that, I was respectful and said "I appreciate the opportunity," but he was saying, "You are not really good enough to draft."

On the other hand, when I was in Miami, Jeff Ireland asked, "Do you think you could be Wes Welker?" I said, "I don't know, but if I have an opportunity, I don't think I could get tackled." I was more confident in my running. I didn't know anything about route running and coverages at the time, but I felt like I could be one of those types of guys. That was a bold statement especially to compare me to a guy like Welk. I didn't realize how hard it really was but I thought, *If he's doing it, I can do it.*

The comparison I heard more often was to Josh Cribbs because he was from Kent and had made a similar conversion. Cribbs was insane. In the back of my mind I thought, *Can I really get to be that good?* But that sense of doubt kind of helped me because I'd think worst-case scenarios and almost start believing guys like Jerry Angelo who said, "You never played the position." Then the competitor kicked in and the confidence came back and I'd say, "Fuck that. I can do that."

The first time I heard from the Patriots was when they called to send out Ivan Fears, the running backs coach. Ivan is one of the greats, and is still our running backs coach.

Coach Fears had me running routes out of the backfield I hadn't run since Pop Warner. Charlie, who also came to all my private workouts, was throwing to me that day. One route I remember Coach Fears having me run was a "return" route where I would run full speed then stop and whip back. Essentially, it was a 5-10-5 short shuttle. We also went outside to field punts but it was freezing rain and wind blowing everywhere. I caught two punts and Coach said, "OK, we need to get the fuck out of here. You can catch a punt."

What was hard was when Coach Fears put me on the whiteboard and quizzed me on plays and formations that were drawn up. I had to tell him all my protections and where my reads were if different things happened. He stumped me. I think he asked what an inverted defense was which means, in technical terms, quarter, quarter, halves defense, the cover-two, field side. I knew that one but it didn't come out right, and I felt like an idiot. Those guys can make you feel stupid really easily, especially a college kid. They want to fluster you and see how you handle it. Coach Martin said, "If you don't know something, you tell them. You don't go and explain something and look like an idiot."

Coach Fears was there to see about my potential as a third-down back and find out if I could scan against certain protections. I didn't get everything right but I had enough raw knowledge to know what was close to right. But at the time, I thought I bombed.

The next week, New England sent out Scotty O'Brien, the special teams coordinator. He wanted to see me catch kick-offs and punts. I was struggling on the punts because he had the kid punting them so they weren't turning over. I didn't know how to read the punt.

Finally, Scotty said, "Hold up, hold up, hold up. Come over here. What's the first thing a punt returner does?" I said, "Check the wind?" He said, "No. You have to check how many guys are on the field to see if you're legal. And you don't know how to read a punt." I said, "No, I don't."

Coach O'Brien told me, "If it's a right-footed punter and the tip comes down when it's descending [that's called "turning over"], you play the ball on your right titty because it's going to go left and long like a spiral. If it doesn't turn over, you play the ball on your left titty and you have to circle it because it's going to go short and to the right."

Once he told me that, I said, "Ohhhhh, that's how you do it." The key to catching punts is to catch them with your feet. Where you go as it's coming down determines if you're going to have an easy catch or not. So he taught me that and I started catching punts.

I really liked Scotty O. He'd been with Coach Belichick in Cleveland, coached with the Panthers, and was with the Patriots as special teams coach through 2014 before moving into scouting. He was a cool guy and we ended up spending a lot of time together.

But I didn't think I'd see him again. The Patriots didn't bring me in for a visit, so I thought that was a bad sign in terms of their interest. In the end, I worked out four or five times and went on three visits. We were counting down to draft day hoping to hear my name called.

I didn't worry too much about the early part of the draft. I knew I would be a second-day guy and I was thinking I had my best shot with Miami. They had success with the Wildcat and my being a dual-threat quarterback who could throw the ball (shittily, but I could throw it) gave me value. As a California kid, I didn't mind the weather there, either.

Then the Dolphins drafted Pat White, a quarterback from West Virginia. Dual-threat guy. Well, there goes Miami. I didn't know what to expect but I had gotten my hopes up, and I let my feelings get hurt by that. On Sunday, we gathered at the house on Highland. It was family and a bunch of buddies, including Jack Williams from Kent, who was with the Broncos at that point. It was getting toward the end of the draft and I was hoping maybe I'd be a Niner. By the end of the sixth round, my phone rang. It was my agent, Don, and he said a bunch of teams were offering priority free-agent contacts. That meant they weren't going to draft me but they wanted me to sign with them and they'd give me like $20,000 or something.

I thought, *Well at least I'll get $20,000 out of this*, even if I wasn't getting drafted. I said to Don, "Where do you think I should go? I'm not really informed on how this works."

We decided on Green Bay. I fit their system, they didn't really have a slot guy, it was a special franchise with history, and who knows? Maybe I'd go to the Packers and be a part of Green Bay history, me and Aaron Rodgers.

As the seventh round started, Don called and said, "You never know, but the Patriots have a couple of seventh-round draft picks. I'm not saying anything, but I wouldn't be surprised if they call."

I was thinking, *They ain't calling. They didn't have me in for a visit. I'm going to be a Packer.*

Then I get a call from a private number. It was Berj Najarian, the director of football and head coach administration for the Patriots. He said, "I wanted to call and let you know we have selected you in the seventh round, pick 232. Here's Bill Belichick."

I walked out the door to get some quiet because everyone was asking, "Who is it? Who is it?"

I'm like, "Yo, be quiet!" I was nervous. I got outside and Coach Belichick gets on the phone and goes, "Hey, this is Coach Belichick. We are going to draft you. We really don't know what you are going to play but we know you can play football. Nancy Meier [the Patriots' director of scouting administration] will call you tonight to get you situated. Have a good one."

That was it. I'd just gotten drafted. It was probably the best day in my life to that point. I'd thought of it when I was a kid, but this was the pinnacle. All my friends were there and they were going crazy.

Then the question popped into my head: "How many guys do they have? Can I make this team?"

Don said, "It's going to be tough, but you're too good a football player so I don't think they'll cut you. You are going to play yourself onto this team, but you have a long way to go. It's no walk in the park here."

Don knew because he'd done all of this with Tom. But while everyone was going nuts and was so proud and yelling, I was obsessing about actually making the team.

TEN

HEY, EDELNUT!

Being drafted by the Patriots meant two things: First, I was part of a legendary franchise and about to be coached by the future Hall of Famer Bill Belichick alongside players like Tom Brady (another surefire Hall of Famer), Wes Welker, and Randy Moss. Second, making the team was going to be the biggest challenge I had ever faced.

I would be lying if I didn't admit to being terrified. I'd never been a receiver, and I was taking reps alongside legends. I'd never been a punt returner, and I knew special teams was the key to making the team. I switched positions at Woodside High my sophomore year and that worked out. And I beat out the competition at the College of San Mateo and Kent State. But this was a whole other level.

Rookie minicamp in early May was my first introduction to the receiver position in an actual practice setting. Flying through drills, having to catch the ball while being contested, catching off the Jugs ball-throwing machine, trying to do one-on-ones and cuts against defenders, I went through a baptism by fire. I was so raw; I didn't even know how to get in a receiver's stance at the line of scrimmage. But my attitude was, "Screw it, let's go!"

The Patriots have a standard in everything they do. I saw and felt it instantly. There is no concept of "good enough." You do things the right way in everything, all the time. It wasn't, "OK, you were close, you tried, good enough, let's move on." The coaching is intense and there was so much I needed to be coached on. But this was what I was raised for. A part of me felt confident because I'd been through it all since I was eight years old. The information and expectations were new. But going from Frank Edelman to Bill Belichick wasn't a big jump in terms of intensity.

Some of my skills translated quickly. My quickness and ability to juke and get separation was there. During one-on-ones, I could sometimes put it all together on a rep, pull something out of my ass and make a corner look silly. But there were more times when I was running around like the Tasmanian Devil I was known for being back home.

The hardest parts for me were conditioning and learning the playbook. My polish as a receiver wasn't going to impress them. My motor had to. I refused to show I was tired, but I was dead. Meanwhile, the playbook was about three-and-a-half inches thick and it was like switching to calculus from arithmetic. It was a lot for me to handle.

The best way for me to learn was to write everything down, then make flashcards. The writing helped me learn and the flashcards made it easy for me to get people to quiz me on all the things that I needed to know. For a receiver, that includes route concepts, formations, protections, adjustments, and depths of routes; the list is truly endless because the playbook is always changing and evolving. Before I flew out for rookie camp, I called our receivers coach, Chad O'Shea, and asked for a list of routes and formations we'd use at the first practice so I'd be prepared. Then I quizzed myself. The change from calling the play as a quarterback in college to hearing it as a receiver in the NFL was harder than I thought. I was used to hearing it from the sidelines or having it signaled to me, I wasn't used to it being spoken to me in the huddle.

I was also in a new area with a bunch of guys I had never met, living in a hotel. Rookies stayed at the Residence Inn in Foxborough over by what used to be the Piccadilly Pub. There was no free time and there was a curfew. I wasn't going out anyway. When I went back to my room, I made flash cards of the formations and the two- and three-man route concepts in which receivers had to work together on timing coming off the line, depth of routes, and functioning as a group.

Sebastian Vollmer ("Seabass") was a big tackle from Germany drafted in the second round from the University of Houston. He hadn't been invited to the Combine that year, either. We bonded over that. Brian Hoyer, an undrafted quarterback from Michigan State, was another guy I got close with right away.

Coach Belichick? Not as much. He was pretty terrifying. One day during rookie camp, we were gathered together and he pointed to a picture. I thought it was one of our guards, Steve Neal, but we had no freaking clue. Bill said, "You're going to be sitting next to a guy that has been playing for seven years and you don't know his name? It would be a good thing to get to know your teammates. So why don't you guys get a printout of everyone on the team and learn their names." Needless to say, I printed out that list and studied it.

Pop ID quizzes and questions about who was in the picture on the door to the meeting room became standard fare for us. Coach was always quizzing. Morning meeting was crazy stressful because you didn't know if you were getting a question. I would be in my seat going over my notes like I was preparing for a test, hoping he wouldn't call on me. That was my first impression of Coach Belichick.

It was important during rookie camp to take advantage of the teaching from all the coaches. Once the vets were integrated, the coaching, the attention, and the reps were going to be split. I grinded. We all did. It was like the movie *Groundhog Day*. I woke up super early, caught the early bus, then sat in the locker room and studied.

After rookie camp came off-season training activities (OTAs) and passing camps before the whole team convened in June for minicamp. I treated every practice like a real game. If I messed something up, I couldn't wait for the next day to come so I could do it better and wipe away the stain.

My first rep with Brady came during an OTA. Tom was coming back from the ACL/MCL tear that cost him virtually the entire 2008 season. I was in awe being in the huddle with him, telling myself, *You gotta look good here.* I went out, ran a decent route, Tom threw it . . . and I dropped it. The ball didn't even hit the ground before I heard Tom say, "We have to catch the ball! Let's fucking go!" I was like, *Oh my God.*

It was a couple of days before I got another rep with Tom. When I did, it was a four-wide package with me and Welker inside and Moss and Joey Galloway outside. It was a blitz-zero, meaning man-to-man coverage with no safety help downfield. I put a move on Brandon Meriweather, one of the starting safeties, broke it off, and made a good little play. I was thrilled—I did something right! I had applied the coaching point, which was, if the weak safety comes close to the line of scrimmage and you're in this formation, you have to stop your route early, "break hot," meaning anticipate being the receiver to get the ball in case of a blitz, and "sight adjust" which means reading where the coverage is and going in the direction that's got the least resistance, or "leverage."

It's funny how you remember all the firsts so easily. The first time I met Tom, for instance, he was coming into the locker room from the team meeting auditorium as I was leaving. Don Yee and Steve Dubin were his agents, too, so he knew who I was. He stuck out his hand and I half-dropped my playbook as I took it. He said something along the lines of, "We are excited to have you and I look forward to working with you." He was probably just being a nice guy. I stammered something about being glad to be there and moved along quickly.

Welker was at the salad bar in the team cafeteria when I first saw him. He was in a sweet leather coat, looking fresh, while all of us rookies were in our sweats and Patriots gear. I was trying to make eye contact with him and strike up a conversation, but there was nothing doing.

Randy Moss I was pretty intimidated by. The guy was a legend, one of the best receivers to ever play the game. I didn't want to walk up to him and have him say, "Who the hell are you?" so I didn't really talk to him at first, but Randy became an awesome teammate. Even in my rookie year, he never really messed with us. He used to call me "Edelnut," as in, "Hey, Edelnut! Go get me a towel!" When he was at Marshall they were in the Mid-America Conference along with Kent State, so I think he identified with me a bit, and he would give me tips on little things like coming out of breaks during my route or using my footwork, because he knew I was in la-la land with what I was doing.

There were so many stars. In the training room I'd see Tedy Bruschi walking around with a putter, reading a damn book. I have my playbook, I'm stressed out about when my next meeting is, and trying to get taped up—a long way from feeling that relaxed and at home.

I was quiet. I was told, "Be seen, not heard." There's a class system in an NFL locker room, and rookies are at the very bottom of it, especially before training camp.

Bruschi noticed me during OTAs. He was taking a rep on the punt team and I was in a blocking spot on the return team. I had to practice my "stab" blocking technique, which is to stab or ward off the opposing player to keep him off-balance while maintaining your leverage, which means keeping your body between the player and the area you're guarding. He ran down the field and I stabbed away at him.

After the rep, he looked at me and said, "Hey, rook. Don't you ever touch me again, all right?" As we lined up for the next rep, I thought about what to do. I wanted to compete as hard as I could, but not piss off Bruschi. So this time, I stabbed the air next to him, around him, under him, anything to avoid touching him. It was absurd and I looked like an idiot, but there wasn't any way around it.

Coach Belichick didn't let me catch punts until halfway through OTAs, when he sent me out with Kevin Faulk, Wes Welker, and Terrence Wheatley. Faulk was a straight pro, so smooth. Coach Belichick told us, "All right, you assholes are going to catch with one hand." I still wasn't even comfortable catching punts with two hands. It was a struggle for me. Faulk and Welker made it look easy. They'd been returning punts forever.

Meanwhile, Welker was a damn machine. Every rep he took was under control. Every move he made was set up by something he'd done leading into it. I didn't know the little things in terms of translating my quickness into running a good route. I didn't realize that on a return route, which is a short route where you cut in, stop, then return to where you made the cut, you needed to point your right foot out at the quarterback, for instance. I'd be too quick and lose leverage because I was running full speed, stopping, then turning on a dime. Wes got open on every play. I couldn't. I was determined to learn because, as hard as it was, there were times I sat at my locker, looked at my helmet and my practice jersey with number 11 on it, and thought, *Damn, this is pretty cool.*

I loved everything about being there. The food, the smoothie bar, free cleats and gloves—it was something I'd been dreaming about since I was a kid. I wasn't sure how long I'd be there, so I drank it all in and would stay at the facility in the tubs until nine or ten at night, studying my playbook. And there was so much to study! Thank God for Scott O'Brien. He gave me opportunities on special teams because I was always volunteering. I was in every special teams meeting for about four years with Scotty O. Kickoff, kickoff return, punt, punt return, field goal, field goal block. If I wasn't on the main team, I was a backup to someone. Scotty put a lot of time into me and we developed a relationship, along with Chad O'Shea, our receivers coach. Both men were in their first season with the Patriots in 2009 after being in the league for several years.

The locker room was loaded with good players, so I knew I had to stand out. I didn't really go anywhere, leaving my hotel only to walk to Piccadilly's. Walking with Seabass or another one of the rookie linemen, Rich Ohrnberger, was the extent of my fun. I hung out with those two, George Bussey, Ron Brace, Myron Pryor, and Jake Ingram. Higher-draft-pick players hung out with other higher-draft-pick players, for the most part. Ingram became a friend because he'd gone to the University of Hawaii, where he played with Polynesians like I had, and we both identified with that culture a bit. When camp came and I met Rob Ninkovich, Ninko became one of my guys, too.

Ninko had bounced around between the Saints and Dolphins since coming into the league in 2006. He was a late-round pick, like me, and his dad was an ironworker. He came to us in early August after being released by the Saints, and I remember watching him go up against Matt Light during a training camp practice. Ninko was a handful in one-on-ones, and Coach Belichick would highlight some of his plays. I went up to him one day and said, "Dude, you're a beast!" and we hit it off from there. We connected. A night out for me was leaving the Residence Inn to hang out with Ninko, Matt Slater, or Tully Banta-Cain, one of our defensive ends who was also from the Bay Area. But I didn't even set foot in Boston until just before the season began. I went to my hotel room almost every day after practice and studied. I was never the best student, and I knew in this course you didn't get a C. You get cut and you go back to being a parts boy at A-1 Auto Tech.

Even though I grew up geographically close to Brady, I wasn't going to bother him with small talk about any of that. Each player is legitimately and completely worried about himself. We'd been going six months strong with combine training and hadn't stopped. We would dick around here and there, but I was there for one reason, to make the team. I had to adjust to so many things. For instance, as a quarterback in college, I wasn't used to hearing the play; I was used to saying it. Now I had to not only listen closely, but also process what it meant for a position I wasn't used to. I would call Dad, completely stressed-out because the ebbs and flows of having a good day and not having a good day were constant. Being consistent was hard when I had to retain new information and then execute it against other guys. If my confidence got shot here and there, I hunkered down and leaned back on what had gotten me there: work.

After minicamp in early June we had a month off before training camp. That period was a farewell to my youth, family, and friends, because I was going on a mission. I had a mountain to climb and I had to prepare myself for that climb. Looking too far into the future and wondering whether I'd make the team stressed me out, so I stayed in the moment and focused on the next thing. Obviously, this wasn't the military, but I tried to take the same approach. You don't have friends, you don't have family, and you don't have fun.

The first day of training camp with fans present blew me away. There were maybe five hundred people at Senior Day when I was at Kent. Here in Foxborough, there were more than ten thousand. New Englanders love their sports, so I was nervous and wanted to make a good impression on everyone. Catching punts before practice, I dropped two and, since I was pretty much the only guy out there doing anything, they booed me! I was competing for a position on the team, and they were calling attention to my screwups.

We had two-a-day practices at camp in 2009, so I was tired most of the time. Rookie year is the toughest by far because you really don't know what you're doing. You're in some new place, you've been training for five months since before your pro day, you took no days off before camp, you've got meetings until eight o'clock at night, you're at the facility late every night, all the while not knowing if that one rep will lead to your getting cut.

Even though I came into the NFL with comparisons to Wes, he didn't take me under his wing, and I didn't expect him to. That's not how it works. I was a rookie trying to get my shit together. Wes was a veteran, three years deep into the system. He had his group of friends and I had mine. It was more of a veteran-rookie thing. As a vet, you don't know if a guy is going to make the team. It's a job and it's competition, so there really wasn't a relationship.

I would ask him questions here and there and he would answer them every once in a while. Sometimes he would say, "Hey, rook, just listen to the fucking coach."

Wes Welker

Julian was definitely raw, especially early on, but his vision from playing quarterback and his quickness stood out. He understood the concepts of route running, too. But the difference between college and the NFL is massive even if you played receiver in college. Guys either understand football and work hard at it or they don't. That's the way it works. Julian was one of those guys who definitely worked his tail off. Right off the bat, first day, he sat at the desk right next to me asking questions. Almost to an annoying point. That's his personality and you would rather have it that way—a guy who takes the bull by the horns and tries to learn—than someone being too shy or scared or prideful to ask a question.

That's what you have to do if you want to get better. I did the same thing with Tim Dwight and Eric Parker when I first got in the league in San Diego. I watched how they prepared, how they ate, how they trained, how they did everything. I kind of mimicked the guys who I felt did it the right way and picked things up along the way. Julian did the same thing with me. He may have had a question about why I did this or that, but if I ran a route and he was the next one in line behind me, watching every single step, he was able to mimic. Trying to explain something and talk through it is not easy. It's almost better to get on the field and walk through the steps and go through instead of saying, "Do this against this and that against that."

I viewed Julian as competition, for sure. You're not good at what you do unless you're competitive. That's the nature of the beast and that's the way it is. That's the way you want it. I know Jules and I made each other better by him pushing me and me being like, "I can't let this guy beat me out" while he tried to beat me out every single day. At the end of the day, you want that on the football team. You want everyone out there with their lives on the line and their jobs on the line and competing every single day. I think that's when teams get really good is when guys are pushing each other to get to that level. You have to get the right guys with that mentality of, "I'm coming out here to compete today."

Patriots fans remember the 2009 season as one of upheaval and personnel change, from players to coaches to the front office. Between the end of the 2008 season and the 2009 opener, Mike Vrabel and Richard Seymour were traded; Rodney Harrison retired in the off-season and Tedy Bruschi retired toward the end of camp; Scott Pioli and Josh McDaniels left for the Chiefs and Broncos, respectively; Jabar Gaffney and Lonie Paxton went to Denver with Josh and Larry Izzo went to the Jets. Prominent among the coaching staff changes was Bill O'Brien taking over offensive playcalling.

Meanwhile, I was so young and naive, I really didn't know shit about what was going on around me. All I knew was that I had a million meetings and I'd better keep them straight or I'd be headed back to Redwood City. By August, I needed to play a game. I was a little out of control. I was going super hard on reps you weren't supposed to go super hard on and hitting guys harder than I was supposed to. Stupidly going one hundred miles per hour at all times, I heard, "Bro, chill the fuck out!" more than once. There was a fine line between learning speed and competition speed, and I was constantly at or over it.

Finally, it was time for the Eagles. August 13, 2009, at Lincoln Financial Field, I was making my NFL debut and Tom Brady would be playing his first game since the previous September, when Kansas City's Bernard Pollard took him down in the opener. People were most interested in Tom's return or the news that was breaking that night about Michael Vick returning to the NFL and joining Philly, but to me and my family and friends, my taking the field was the biggest news on the planet. I didn't care if it was preseason, this was an experience I was going to hold on to. If something went wrong and I got cut, at least I'd be able to say I'd gotten one NFL game under my belt.

At the last second, I found out Wes wasn't playing and I was out there with the starters at wide receiver, Randy Moss and Joey Galloway. I got into things early, making the tackle on the opening kickoff. On our first possession of the night, I caught Tom's first pass since the injury, a little six-yarder. On our next drive, I caught another five-yarder. It didn't seem real; Tom Brady was throwing to *me*.

With 11:27 left in the first half, I went out to field my first NFL punt. The Eagles' punter Sav Rocca hit a high hanger to me that I fielded at our 22. I scrambled around a little and didn't get anything. From the sideline, I heard Tom yell, "Get upfield!" I thought, *This motherfucker, he's never even done this before.* I was pissed but . . . flag. The Eagles were called for illegal formation. We made them punt again.

This time, Rocca's punt led me over to the right sideline. Drifting under it, I remembered what Scotty O. always told me: "Keep your hands high and your elbows in and watch the ball." I pulled it in at the 25 and took a quick survey. There was room and I had blocking. A little shimmy at our 30 freed me up. I stuck my right foot in the ground at their 45 and cut sharply to my left and that was it. Nothing good ever happens for a punt coverage team when it has to kick twice. They were too tired. The Eagles basically stopped chasing me by the time I got to their 30.

I was so juiced, so happy, as I crossed the goal line. I wound up and threw the ball right against the end wall! I had so much fury and passion and joy, and thinking of all the people who said I wasn't ever going to be able to do anything, I was like, "Fuck you!" Randy came up and gave me a big old hug, and one of our corners, Darius Butler, was there and we did a chest bump. I was so fired up I went and sat on the bench and tried to process it. I had to make plays in the preseason and I knew I'd made one.

I learned later that Coach Belichick called into his headphones to Ernie Adams, the team's football research director and a man who's known Coach since prep school. Coach Belichick asked, "Hey Ernie, what was the name of that guy that played before Lou Gehrig?" When he had the answer he went to Wes and said, "You ever heard of Wally Pipp? You never heard of him? Well he played first base before Lou Gehrig. Gehrig came in for Pipp and started like twenty-three thousand straight games." Wes just smiled, not knowing who Wally Pipp was. "That might be our punt return story." Wes smiled and said, "Hey, he can have it, man. Make a play like that . . ."

Then Bill said, "Aw, there ya go. Way to compete."

To me, Wes was untouchable. He was a technician and I didn't know how to do anything yet. I was too raw and I knew it, but I felt like I could make stuff happen if I had the ball in my hands. As far as being a receiver Wes was a machine. I was still trying to run an L-route. It was cool, though. After the game, I was on the bus, still excited as we were going over the bridge to New Jersey. We could see the stadium out the window and I was sitting next to Brian Flores, a new coach who has become a terrific defensive coach for us. It was his first game, too, and we were like, "Our first game is behind us."

Wes Welker

I didn't know who Bill was talking about with the Wally Pipp and Lou Gehrig comment. I didn't even really think anything of it. I didn't look it up. It wasn't until after it aired that people told me about what it was all about. I was just like, "OK." I kind of got what he meant because Julian had just returned a punt for a TD. He was saying, "Way to compete," but come on! Like I'm not going to compete. You don't have to even tell me that! That's Bill being Bill, no doubt.

Matt Slater

Having been around this team a long time, I can honestly say that I have never seen a rookie come in with the mind-set that Julian came in with in 2009. His desire to compete was second to none. He was just hungry to have some stats and do whatever it took to have some success, and that really caught my eye.

The play from the Eagles game that jumped out to me wasn't the punt return, it was the opening kickoff. This kid came down full speed, didn't break stride, and just threw his body into the returner. I thought to myself, "There is something different about this guy." I watched him compete. If there was a drill, Jules would get in line right behind Wes. If Wes ran a route, Julian was right behind him to run the route right after him. That really struck me. He was there with one of the greatest receivers in the history of the organization, and he wasn't afraid to compete with Wes. I think that is a unique thing about Julian, no question.

When you hear of a team drafting a quarterback with the plan to change his position, automatically you think, "Well, how is this going to happen? Is he going to be afraid of contact?" You wonder how that's going to go. It was really impressive early on what he was able to do, the routes he was able to run as a guy who had never played the position or never had any exposure to the level of play out there. To compete early on with some already established guys in that room, I think that shows the God-given ability Julian has and who he is as an athlete. That willingness to compete—a lot of which he got from his dad—was displayed every day in training camp.

The standard of discipline and accountability and the demand for consistency with the Patriots was one I'd never seen. You adjust quickly or you're not there. One day Coach Belichick spoke to me, a raw rookie, about catching punts because I was struggling. He said, "You catch the punt with your feet." He went over the whole thing with me, even though Scotty had already taught me that. He spent some time with me, forty-five seconds or something, but it made a huge impression. I got a high any time he noticed me or he ran a positive highlight while going over certain film or coaching points. Those little things, that was what I worked for. I did a thousand things wrong, but that one time I heard him say something decent, that made my day. That meant I'd met the standard. I took pride in being a Patriot even before I made the team.

My concern about making the team grew, though, during the second preseason game. I had a couple of modest punt returns and caught one pass for three yards. On one of them, I made a weird cut on the turf and my ankle gave. I sprained it. It was the last thing I needed. It kept me out for the rest of the preseason.

I was still attending meetings but I couldn't do anything else but rehab. Billy O'Brien would always mess with me, saying, "If you're still here when we play Buffalo in the opener . . ." I was terrified. One of our equipment guys, Murph, saw me sitting at my temporary locker late one night and said to me, "Oh, you're still here, huh? They'll get ya . . ." I thought, *Oh my God, I'm going to get cut.*

Cutdown day is the worst. You don't know how things will go, and it all depends on what the coaches think is best. Guys who are versatile help themselves by becoming more valuable, and I guess that's what happened with me. The team kept me on and let go of a veteran receiver named Greg Lewis. Nobody calls to say, "You made the team," they call only if you get cut. So I spent the day walking around checking my phone, dreading the moment I'd get a blocked call.

I spent a lot of the year preparing for the worst-case scenario of being sent home. As a result, I never got an apartment. Instead, I lived in the basement of one of our linebackers, Pierre Woods. I was tight with my money. I think the biggest purchase I made was an Xbox. I didn't want to jinx myself.

After I'd made the team, my folks came out to spend a weekend in Boston. It was similar to when they dropped me off at Kent, but this time there were no separation tears from Mom, just pride. It was a new chapter. We went on a duck boat tour and had dinner downtown at the Capital Grille. It turned out Junior Seau was there that night and he came up to my parents, shook their hands and said, "Mr. and Mrs. Edelman, you really raised a good son." That was a thrill for all of us.

My ankle kept me out of the season opener against Buffalo but Tom brought us back in his return to the field after a year away. We came back from being eleven points down with five minutes left to win 25–24. I watched from home/ Pierre's living room, and while I was glad to be a part of that team, I also thought, *I've got to get my shit together or I'm not going to be playing next week, either.*

Wes couldn't play the following week in New York because of a knee injury. It was our first game against the Jets since Rex Ryan had taken over, and the lead-in to that game was all about the stuff Rex was talking about taking on the Patriots.

Coach does a good job of keeping our heads out of the headlines so I wasn't worried about that. Now, as a starter, I was just trying not to mess up anything we put into the game plan. Both Chad O'Shea and Nick Caserio, who preceded Chad as receivers coach before moving over to the personnel side of the team, went over the whole call sheet with me and tested me on where I was supposed to line up. That's about 180 plays. We were going no-huddle that game and it was going to be loud (Rex actually sent a message to all season ticket holders during the week to make sure they made noise) so we were using wristbands to help with nonverbal communication.

It was a rough game. We lost 16–9 and even though I had eight catches for ninety-eight yards, there was so much shit I could have done better. I definitely didn't feel like I'd made it. I wasn't a big part of things for the next few games until a snowy game against Tennessee on October 18, when I made six catches, but most of those came after the game turned into a 59–0 blowout. The team was in flux that year. I didn't know any different as a rookie, because I had no frame of reference, but the departure of so many important players in one off-season had left the team adrift in terms of leadership. It was a mix of the players who'd won Super Bowls and been there for the foundational years of the dynasty and players who'd joined the team after that success. Now I can see the difference. We were up and down and were trying to find an identity. My contributions against the Titans came with a price. I broke my arm when Tennessee's Kyle Vanden Bosch landed on my arm after a screen pass. When I went down, all our combined weight landed on it.

I missed two games and thought I was going to miss the game in Indy against the Colts, too, because the injury kept me out of practice all week. Saturday, before we left, Coach Belichick came to me and said, "Get a suit, you're coming with us."

Matt Slater was my roommate, and I was up all night worried about whether I'd be able to play because of how my arm felt. Sunday morning when I woke up, I said, "Wait, it's

Sunday Night Football in Indy, of course I'm going to play." I was there primarily as a backup in case anyone went down anyway, with a small package of plays that I was involved in. One of them was in the red zone, and that's when I caught my first real NFL touchdown: a nine-yard scramble from Tom in the first half to put us up 24–7. I was stoked, but the arm was messed up so I had to spike it with my left hand. I ran and jumped on Tom and he said, "Yeah, great. We still have a lot of game left, buddy."

We sure did. That was the game that Coach Belichick decided to go for it on fourth-and-2 from our own 21 late in the game. There was a lot of discussion outside the team about that because we didn't pick it up and the Colts scored on a Peyton Manning–to–Reggie Wayne touchdown pass with thirteen seconds left and took a 35–34 win. I learned in that game that no lead is safe in this league and that, no matter what, Coach Belichick has balls. I've learned to never question him, because being around him, you know how it works. His mind is like a computer and his decision making might be risky at times but he's got an amazing feel for the game. It won't always work, but he does things for a reason.

I was targeted only six times in the next four games before we headed into our season finale at Houston. I remember that game like it was yesterday. I jogged onto the field with Wes and I asked him what it felt like, playing back in Texas after playing in college at Texas Tech and being one of the baddest receivers in the league. He kind of shrugged me off. Then, on our first drive, he planted his foot in the turf and tore his ACL. I didn't have time to feel bad for him, even though I knew how upset he was. I was supposed to replace him. There couldn't be a drop-off.

I wound up having my first 100-yard game—103 yards on ten catches—but it was a pretty sloppy game. Now we were headed into the playoffs without Wes and there was a lot of focus on me to perform. As a team we were uneven at best. But I was happy to be going into the playoffs. I hadn't been in a postseason game since the College of San Mateo, a chance to be part of a team that wins it all is what every player works for. We would face the Ravens at Gillette Stadium. With Ed Reed, Ray Lewis, Terrell Suggs, Haloti Ngata, Chris McAlister, and a bunch of other guys, they were a hard-nosed team and a tough draw. They were students of the game, too. They didn't just play fast and physical, they were smart and not afraid to take chances.

It was one of those days for us. Baltimore jumped on us and went up 24–0 in the first quarter. I scored both our touchdowns—one on a six-yarder in the first half and a one-yard catch late in the third—but we lost 33–14. But no one remembers if you played well when you lose. I did gain some confidence through the season, but the feeling afterward reminded me of Kent State. We knew we were a better team than we showed, but what matters is how you play.

I was pretty beat up by the end of the year. In addition to my broken arm, I needed off-season surgery for a sports hernia and a mild groin tear that were discovered after the season. But I was determined to build on the way I played at the end of the year once everything was cleaned up. I needed to improve at everything.

ELEVEN

SCRATCHING TO STICK

Coach Belichick talks about the jump players make from their first year to their second. I definitely felt more confident and better understood what was expected of me. After coming to the NFL not knowing how to play wide receiver or return punts, I had a productive rookie year. Including the playoffs, the numbers were 43 catches for 403 yards and three touchdown catches, as well as 11 punt returns averaging 9 yards each.

Gains come in the off-season, though, so I said to my agents, "Wherever Brady is going to work out, I want to be near there." Tom sometimes threw with Wes and Randy in Los Angeles, so Don and Carter set me up near Manhattan Beach in a Residence Inn on the Pacific Coast Highway. I drove my parents' old Jeep Cherokee down from Redwood City and waited for a call from Brady.

He called. Once. And I was pretty sure it was because he had no one else to throw to. It was a Friday afternoon and I was at a barbecue in Marina del Rey and he called. I said, "Gotta go!" We went to UCLA. I was there about a half hour early getting warmed up, and he ran me into the ground.

That was the first time I got a sense of how hard he trains in the off-season.

With Wes still rehabbing from his ACL injury, there were plenty of reps for me during OTAs and passing camps. I was still raw, but I felt there was a little more faith in me around the coaching staff, although Tom still wasn't totally comfortable with me. As far as I'd come, I certainly wasn't Wes. And Wes returned from the knee injury in surprising time and was back working with Tom. He was a beast.

Changes were made after the disappointing end to 2009. The defense turned over: Adalius Thomas, Shawn Springs, and Jarvis Green were all gone. Laurence Maroney and Benjamin Watson were gone on offense. During the draft, the team made a move to stock up the tight end position with Rob Gronkowski and Aaron Hernandez. You could tell immediately that they were talented players, and throughout that off-season, our scheme was designed to take advantage of them.

Before the rest of the team even met Gronk, we were hearing from the coaches that he was a little different. Billy O. just kept saying, "You are gonna love this guy. He's a beauty." Billy was right. Gronk was this big ball of energy and childlike innocence. He was amazed by the simplest things. But people have no idea how smart he is. On the field, playing one of the most complex positions in our offense, he never made mistakes.

The first time I went out with Gronk in Boston was probably the last time I could go out with him without being recognized. A few of us, including Gronk and Tully Banta-Cain, went out to a club in Boston, and before long Gronk was on the floor, dress shirt unbuttoned down to his stomach, dancing around like a big ogre. People were asking, "Who's that guy?" I said, "That's Gronk. You'll get to know him."

The team put a lot of special teams work on my plate that off-season. I was with Scotty O. for more special teams meetings, even the units I wasn't on. I was trying to add value any way I could, and I always felt like Scotty liked me. I was hungry to learn, and he'd tell me about the great punt returners he'd worked with—Eric Metcalf in Cleveland and Steve Smith in Carolina—and he'd run film of them to teach me.

We had so many meetings because I knew that if I was going to make the team I had to do well on special teams. I spent countless hours my first few years with Scotty O. talking football and watching film. I'd get the video cutups of the most productive punt returners and we'd watch them together. I'd pause the film just as the returner caught it to see how he went from tracking the ball to getting upfield and making people miss. That's the thing about punt returns: you're so reliant on your blockers and knowing the scheme of the play and understanding where the most blockers are. I learned to take a still shot of where everyone was when the ball left the punter's foot. Then I learned to track the punt, catch it cleanly with my feet being aligned so I was able to go to either direction, instead of catching it to the side. I learned how to process where there would be a lane and how to set up a move to get where you need to be going. Watching the great returners, I learned how to set up blocks, how to get vertical, how to track when you are getting upfield. I learned hang times and understanding the depths of punts. I learned which situations allowed you to catch the ball inside the 5-yard line and which situations allowed you to catch the ball past the 8-yard line. Scotty O. prepared me for all these things.

He also taught me how to be the personal punt protector—the guy on the punt team who stands in front of the punter as the last line of defense. I learned protections, how to cover kicks, and figure out where guys could be coming from to potentially knock your head off.

We developed a relationship that went beyond football. Scotty loved cars, and he would talk to me about that because he knew my dad was a mechanic. He'd talk about his dad, who'd been a boxing trainer. He was crazy as hell, but I was kind of like his puppy. He'd yell at me hard when I made a shitty play! I'd hear him as I came to the sideline, "*You son of a bitch!*" Then a minute later, he'd come over, put his arm around me, and say, "Every play's an experience. Remember that."

It helped. Our first preseason game was against the Saints, and my first punt return was for forty yards. Between that and a six-catch, ninety-yard game, and my improved ability to line up quickly and understanding my job on each play, I had a good start to the year. *This could be a good year,* I thought.

A week later, my preseason was over. Playing the Falcons in the Georgia Dome, I brought in a pass from Tom on third-and-9 late in the first quarter and felt my foot stick in the turf. Sprained foot. I didn't have enough on my résumé to be missing preseason games, and this would be the second year in a row I wasn't going to finish training camp. Sometimes durability is better than ability, and I wasn't showing it.

Meanwhile, the offense evolved drastically through the preseason and into the regular season. The team traded Randy to Minnesota in early October and brought back Deion Branch. Kevin Faulk tore his ACL and was replaced by Danny Woodhead. BenJarvus Green-Ellis became the lead back instead of Fred Taylor. I missed the opener because of my foot and caught four passes in the next two games. After that, not one catch until the season finale, when I had three catches after the starters exited in a blowout of Miami. I was a spare part folded into the mix here and there.

It was tough—in my first game in the NFL in 2009, I had nine catches and didn't even know what I was doing. To finish my second season with seven? I was losing ground on offense, so I put everything I had into special teams.

There is an urgency that professional athletes feel when they see how close they are to getting cut. To stay on a team, you have to make plays, of course. When the opportunities are limited, you go into survival mode. Every kick I covered, I flew down like a missile. Every chance to make a return, I took it. I ended up averaging 15.3 yards on 21 returns, which was good, but the train will leave without you if you're not on it.

There are no guaranteed contracts in the NFL. If you're not on the field, you better do everything you can to get back, because the person who replaced you might make you expendable. Coach Belichick says that you earn your role. I took that to heart. Yes, I was pissed off that I wasn't playing offense. But, shit, I was a college quarterback. Who was I to have an ego? My approach was to do anything to get on the field, so I embraced special teams, though of course I didn't really have a choice. Nobody cared what I'd done the year before. It's a business. Are you available to contribute today? That's the mentality.

If I didn't understand that, Randy being traded made it very clear. That was when I thought, *Holy crap! They don't care what your name is here. If you don't perform, you're gone. If they're trading Randy Moss, nobody's safe.* Anyone feeling a little loose and comfortable at that point had his ass pucker up quick.

It was an honor to play with Randy. He looked out for the underdogs and the rookies. Back then, rookies occasionally had to buy lunch for the whole position group. And it wasn't a $40 tab at Subway. It would end up being $300 or more from a restaurant. Luckily for me, while I still had to pick up lunch,

Randy would give me the money to buy it. He made me feel comfortable. Maybe a little too comfortable. He was at his locker the previous December and was talking with his mom. I walked past and said, "Hey Randy! Tell Mama Moss I said Merry Christmas!"

Randy took the phone away from his mouth and said, "Hey, Edelman! When I'm talking to my motherfucking mom, you shut the fuck up!" I realized maybe I wasn't *that* cool with him. But he really cared about teammates, especially the ones on the fringes, and that was me.

But the team that was 16-0 in 2007 with Randy setting an NFL record with 23 touchdown receptions was gone by 2010. Gronkowski and Hernandez were at the leading edge of change on offense. Gronk was a beast. At six foot six, 265 pounds, he played with an attitude that said, "I'm going to run you over and there's nothing you can do about it." That physical style and the joy he took in playing made him seem like a big kid out there. And Hernandez, "Chico," was one of the best route runners I've ever seen. He had a basketball style in which he'd stop and start or use his shoulders to set up crossover steps. His ability to change speeds, to cut back across the pursuit of the defense and accelerate made him unique. It was like something I'd never seen from someone who was six foot one and a power-packed 245 pounds. He was a great player and we got along. Aaron was a student of the game, studying hard, working hard. We'd battle in practice on special teams when he was on punt coverage and I was on punt return. I had a huge respect for the guy because he was a revolutionary kind of player in terms of the things he could do and his versatility. He lined up in the backfield at running back, as a slot receiver working the middle of the field, as a wide receiver running routes outside the numbers, and as a conventional tight end.

The work we were putting in on punt returns was finally rewarded in the last game of the year. We'd been close to breaking one a few times—Detroit's punter tripped me up on Thanksgiving—but the ninety-four-yarder was a good way to end that regular season. Miami's punter, Brandon Fields, out-kicked the coverage. Following two terrific blocks, I cut from the left sideline to the middle of the field and was gone. After a season in which I hadn't made many offensive contributions, I felt great to put some points on the board on special teams.

We finished that season 14-2. Our only losses were week 2 at the Jets and a week 9 loss when we laid an egg in Cleveland. For a team that was rebuilding on the fly after a tough 2009, it was a remarkable accomplishment. As the number one seed, we had a bye for the first round of the playoffs. In the divisional round, we got the Jets. We'd beaten them 45–3 barely a month earlier on *Monday Night Football*. But they still had a potent defense and had been in the AFC Championship the year before. Being in our division, they knew us as well as we knew them. And Rex Ryan knew how to get them up for games.

To me, Rex was entertaining. I thought the stuff he said was pretty funny, WWE kind of material. It didn't bother us. Coach Belichick doesn't want any distractions, though, and he knew that if we said anything, there'd be headlines.

Leading into the game, Wes spoke to the media at his locker and made a collection of foot references. It was clear he was referencing an episode from earlier in the year in which it became clear that Rex was an admirer of his wife's feet. As Coach Belichick sees it, our job is to win football games, not entertain the media or create story lines. He said he didn't want any distractions, and he considered that a distraction, so he threw the book at Wes and I started the game. There wasn't any announcement that I'd be starting. There was chatter around the locker room like in the game "telephone," where we heard bits and pieces but never knew exactly what was going on unless Bill said it. The night before the game, Chad O'Shea mentioned something to the effect that I needed to be ready and if we opened with a certain personnel group I'd probably be out there for the first few plays, but there was no big announcement.

Whether Wes was out there at the start or not didn't decide the game. We'd had a shitty week of practice leading up to it, and the Jets punched us in the mouth and beat us 28–21. It was a bad end to what had been a good season for the team. As Deion Branch said after the game, "We picked the wrong game, the wrong time to play bad football." The Jets reveled in beating us in front of our fans just weeks after we'd hammered them, and they made sure to let everyone know how much that meant to them.

As crushing as it was to have the season end like that, we had a sense that we'd built something in 2010. On the whole, we didn't feel that we were a long way off from being the team we wanted to be. We had a lot of young players gain valuable experience on offense and defense that year. But we had it brought home hard how badly it hurts when you don't show up in the most important game of the year. That was the message Coach Belichick left us with.

Personally, I'd shown value as a returner, but my role in the regular offense was limited. This was going to be another important off-season for me.

TWELVE

A CAREER CROSSROADS

I'm a person who thrives on structure and routine. I like to know where to be, when to be there, and what to do when I get there. I don't like uncertainty, and the early part of 2011 was full of it. The collective bargaining agreement between the NFL's owners and players expired March 11, and with no new agreement on the horizon the owners locked us out. That left us players to fend for ourselves, and it's probably not a coincidence that I wound up having my worst season in the NFL. I learned a lot about myself that year, and by the end, I realized I had some growing up to do or I'd be out of the league for good.

For the off-season, I went back to Southern California for the second straight year to train and be near Tom if he needed a throwing partner. This time, I lived in a condo on Driftwood Street in Marina del Rey with Lucas Yancey (the "Whaboom!" guy from the 2017 season of the *Bachelorette*, remember?) and four other buddies. I was twenty-five years old, living on the beach, hanging out in Venice, and trying to enjoy life, but there was uncertainty surrounding that off-season. For one thing, we were on our own for training, so

I went to my main spot, API (now called EXOS) in Carson, California.

I also worked with Alex Guerrero that off-season. Alex is Tom's body coach and partner at TB12 Sports Therapy. His talent for helping athletes attain peak condition through massage, diet, pliability, supplementation, and hydration is legendary. I figured if it was good enough for Tom, it was definitely good enough for me, and Tom was with Alex 24/7.

I tripled my number of UCLA throwing sessions with Tom from the summer before, bringing me to a grand total of three. But I trained plenty at API, and that's where I first met Danny Amendola. Dola was with the Rams at the time and we competed during training. One day, we walked down the pier afterward, shot the shit, and learned we were in similar situations. He'd had a big year in 2010 with the Rams but was originally an undrafted guy out of Texas Tech who bounced around. We were both trying to stick in the league. We bonded a bit, rode skateboards, biked, and went out for beers after training.

The lockout didn't trip me out. I couldn't control it, so I focused on training and getting better. That off-season, I began watching film of receivers in similar situations to mine, like Victor Cruz from the Giants and the Steelers' Antonio Brown. Victor barely played in 2010, his rookie season, but I knew he was from the University of Massachusetts and had had a very good preseason before his rookie year. Same thing with Antonio. He was a rookie in 2010 who was a sixth-round choice from Central Michigan. I watched them to see what adjustments they were making to the league. Both players had really good, quick feet and, as it turned out, both of them had huge 2011 seasons. With them, every step had a purpose and there was no wasted motion. I also watched film of Dola because he was so productive for the

Rams. I became more comfortable with my footwork but I still wasn't running enough routes with Tom to establish the necessary trust.

Tom is very demanding in how he wants things done and he has been pissed off at a lot of receivers through the years. Since I wore number 11 and Tom wears 12, I lockered next to him my first few seasons in the league, and being close to him each day I gained insight into where he was coming from as we talked about his expectations after practices. We created more of a relationship each year, but I was still in awe of him and his preparation and professionalism. He loved chewing out the Edeldog when I messed up, no doubt, but when we were at our lockers later he would say, "I yell at you because I care about you. If I don't yell at you, you should be worried."

Lockering next to Tom gave me a chance to peek over to my right and see what he was all about, like a little brother keeping an eye on an older brother for cues. The clothes were always a learning experience. Once, I was feeling a little comfortable with him, and I saw he was wearing a pair of jeans that were ripped up and had paint splotches or something on them. I said, "Hey, Tom, you just finish painting your fence or what?" He looked at me and said, "Jules, these pants right here cost more than everything you're wearing and everything you have at home in your closet." He said it with a smile but he made his point. I was too cheap at that point to wear anything but shitty-ass clothes, but Brian Hoyer, who lockered to my left, used to buy a crazy amount of suits and try to look like Tom. That James Bond look Tom had going, I filed it away for later when maybe I had some money.

The lockout wore on that summer and we players did our best to stay organized. We had about forty guys in early June show up for a couple of days of workouts at Boston College. We also had some under-the-radar workouts around Foxborough, all of which were great, but when both sides reached agreement on a new CBA on July 25 we were all relieved.

It was definitely a bittersweet time for us. Our owner, Robert Kraft, had been instrumental in getting the lockout resolved. I'll never forget how he put himself on the line and how hard he worked throughout that period. Meanwhile, his wife, Myra, was battling cancer. The sadness he was dealing with as he went from her bedside to conduct business then back to her bedside was moving. Mrs. Kraft passed away five days before the lockout ended. It was such a blow for all of us. She was so caring and had taken so much time to get to know us as people and cultivate an interest in who we were. I was so sad for all the Krafts because the Patriots are an organization that very much treats its players as family.

The first time I met Mrs. Kraft was at our Kickoff Gala before the 2009 season. I was a little intimidated—you don't want to make the wrong first impression on the owner's wife—but the feeling she gave off was warm and welcoming. If she knew me, she barely knew me, but her warmth and calm were contagious. That's why the philanthropic spirit we've got in our organization is so strong, I believe. It's a very high priority to the Kraft family, and it filters down to the players because of that. Mr. Kraft tells the story that, when he wanted to buy the Patriots in 1993, Mrs. Kraft stressed that she would support him if they pledged to better the community. And the Patriots Charitable Foundation has done that.

With the lockout over, we were at the facility the next day. The day after that, we had a new receiver: Chad Ochocinco. At that point, I saw the number of receivers we had and realized that we were still bringing people in and thinking it could be my last year with the Patriots. It was going to be tough to hang on.

I know it didn't go as well for Ocho as everyone expected, but that guy had unbelievable footwork and was a cool guy, a fun guy to be around. The system is not always easy for some guys to pick up, though. The play called in the huddle can change when you get to the line based on what the defense is in. It can change again *after* the ball is snapped because our routes are often dictated by how the defense reacts once the play begins. There are contingencies—if this happens, you do this; if that happens, you do that—and you have to be more than athletic; you have to be adaptable and able to retain a lot of information. If you aren't seeing things the same way Tom sees them and you go to a spot he's not expecting you to be in, he's not coming to you. Do that often enough, and he loses trust in you. That's just how it is. But Ocho had beautiful feet. He ran an unbelievable comeback route. He ran a post-in where he'd accelerate up on the defensive back—"get up on his toes," we call it—then round it quick with no wasted motion while the DB was still retreating. It was like he could put them on skates. He was a good route runner, the problem was that we didn't always run the same route in our system.

As camp went along, it was clear my opportunities on special teams were again vital to my sticking around. With Gronk and Chico at tight end, Wes and Deion at wide receiver, plus Tiquan Underwood and Taylor Price added at wideout, there weren't enough reps there.

I was dealing with another preseason ding that year as well after I hurt my hand against Jacksonville. I played in two of the four preseason games but my role was expanded from being primarily a punt returner to taking back kickoffs, too. We won at Miami on Monday night, and while I had a solid night on special teams, Tom was incredible, throwing for 517 yards, including a 99-yard touchdown pass to Wes. The offense didn't let up in week 2, a 35–21 win over San Diego as

Tom threw for 423. Our next game was in Buffalo, and it was a very un-Patriot game. We were up 21–0 on the Bills before losing a heartbreaker in the final seconds. We followed up that loss with a trip to Oakland on October 2. It was good to be back in the Bay Area. I got off a couple of decent returns and we beat the Raiders, but I turned an ankle and missed the following games against the Jets, Cowboys, and Steelers. The Steelers game was on October 30. The next night, my career took a nasty turn.

When you're a rookie, you sit through all the meetings and hear all the stories about guys who get arrested and screw up their careers. I would hear those stories and think, *Hey, those guys were stupid. I'm not stupid. That won't happen to me.* Well, it did. I went out on Halloween and judged a costume contest at a nightclub. The potential of bad things happening when you mix late hours with alcohol and the club scene is through the roof. I was arrested that night and accused of improperly touching a woman on a dance floor.

The charges were later dropped, but that night, as I was taken to jail, a million things were going through my head. *What will my parents think? Will I have a job in the morning?* It was a very, very embarrassing moment in my life, to be arrested and in jail. My friend Ben Rawitz bailed me out of jail the next morning. He brought me a suit, helped me find an attorney, and took me back later in the day to my court appearance. It was an awful day. I remember riding around with Ben, not talking much. I thought *Holy smokes. My life is done.* Everything we were told not to do in terms of being out, being in nightclubs, drinking, I'd gone against. Everything I'd worked so hard for was suddenly in jeopardy.

I went directly from court to Coach Belichick's office. I was ashamed and terrified. Bill was actually pretty fatherly through the whole process, which somehow made me feel even worse for letting him down. After leaving Bill's office, I went directly to Mr. Kraft.

Being in our owner's office, I realized that every action and decision I made wasn't just about me, it reflected on the people who believed in me and gave me an opportunity. When you're in the news, it's not "Julian Edelman" it's "Julian Edelman of the New England Patriots." Mr. Kraft made it very clear that he took situations like this personally. He was supportive but there was no "It's OK . . ." tone to the conversation. Regardless of the details of the situation, I had put myself there in the first place.

There's also embarrassment when you walk into the locker room and see your teammates. You've been in a situation that shows less than full commitment to what the goals of the team are. You've created a distraction.

When I went back to the stadium on Wednesday, Bill sat me down and told me I'd be fined. He also said, "You're on a short leash. You're at a crossroads. You're in year three. Next year is year four, last year of your rookie contract. Where are you going to go from here? You better start getting really good at a lot of things or dominant at one thing."

I called my agents, Don and Carter, who were in China for business. They both took it as an opportunity to explain the need to refocus and understand what was directly ahead of me. Did I want to give away everything I'd worked for since I was eight because I was a guy who caused distractions?

That week, I practiced with a fire under my ass, but when we played the Giants, I was awful. I fumbled a punt away in the third quarter and I could hear the boos. It was a low time in my life, probably the lowest I've ever been, especially after losing 24–20 in the final minute. People don't realize that players are not robots, we're humans, and when we're dealing with stress, it's hard to perform. I had some serious mental battles that week between feeling bad about the entire situation, concern about it going forward, and wanting to make up for it on the field somehow. When that week ended, more than anything else, I understood I could not keep being the same guy.

Robert Kraft

That was the only time I remember seeing Julian really, really low. You could see it on his face. When he was talking to me, he had a sheepish look. He really couldn't look me in the eye. I said, "Look, Julian. I was once your age and I never got the chance to be a professional football player as you are now. But I can tell you, as the owner of the franchise, that you're carrying my family name. And when you are involved in something such as this, you are embarrassing me and this whole franchise and everything we stand for." He was really shaken up. Sometimes events like that can be turned into positives if you manage them correctly. I explained to him that there's a saying in the Old Testament that basically explains how one can take a bad situation and turn it into something very positive. I said, "I hope that this situation drills you right between the eyes and does it for you."

At that time, I was living with Matthew Slater and Shane Vereen. There's no one I have more respect for than Slates and having him to lean on made all the difference in the world for me.

Matthew Slater

That incident was an unfortunate situation for all parties involved. When you encounter those situations, you have two options. You can continue and go down the path that you're going down, or you can stop and think, "Why did I end up in this situation to begin with?" and use it as a lesson to grow. That is what I tried to challenge Julian to do at that time. As humans, we are all going to make mistakes, that is inevitable. How you handle them and how you proceed from them is what truly matters. I encouraged him to think about who he was and the direction he was headed in. It was tough for both of us. I was there for him going through that, and I know that he was at a time in his career when things weren't going the way he necessarily wanted them to go. It was a time for him to really step back and say, "Hey, what am I doing here?" He sprung forward from that incident and become a better man and a better professional, and he has grown a lot from it.

The next week we were playing the Jets, and the season took another unexpected twist. On Wednesday, our secondary coach Josh Boyer came to me and said, "You're gonna sit in on our meeting this week. We're low on guys." A run of injuries at cornerback and safety had pushed our secondary depth to its limits. I was an "In Case of Emergency, Break Glass" solution. I was excited because it gave me an opportunity to get on the field. I take pride in being a football player and buckling up the chin strap and playing whenever necessary. And believe it or not, I picked Brian Hoyer a couple of times in practice.

I threw myself into it. After all that happened on Halloween, I welcomed it. It was something to lose myself in, something to take me away from the stress I was feeling. I was holding on for dear life in the league, I felt. To be honest, playing defense didn't feel uncomfortable to me. Some stuff was new. I hadn't backpedaled since Pop Warner, but I was at least familiar with offensive concepts and how plays unfold. I wasn't doing anything great, but I was able to hold my own.

Late in the game against the Jets I squared up against LaDainian Tomlinson on a third-and-6 and took out his legs. He actually got hurt on the play. I felt a little bad, and it was different to be on the giving end instead of the receiving end, where I'd been my whole career. Coming out of that game, I felt like I'd been thrown a life preserver, and the water was up to my neck. I had all that shit going on, I'd been injured, I had seven catches the year before, and I was going to end this season with four. I was trying everything I could to survive, and the chance to play defense was just what I needed.

Because I had experience at both quarterback and receiver, I was a little ahead on the learning curve as a defensive back. I understood the concepts of plays and could cheat a little when I saw certain formations or the play design in the split seconds after the snap. And because I knew what receivers don't like—being grabbed, for instance—I played as physically as I could. My approach was, "What would I be trying to do if I was running this route?" Then I would try to disrupt that.

During practices, I always tried to cover Wes. He was the best, so I figured that would be the best preparation. I'd grab him and hold him and generally piss him off until he'd say, "Stop cheatin', bro! You're fucking cheatin'!"

Now I was in defensive meetings, offensive meetings, special teams meetings. It was a heavy workload, but I was elated to be as busy as I suddenly was. More than anything, I really wanted to get an interception. When I was out there in our dime defense over the next few games, I kept thinking, *Please let this guy mess up and throw it to me.* I knew that in 2004 when Troy Brown played defensive back because of a similar run of injuries, he intercepted Drew Bledsoe. I wanted to match that so bad. Playing defensive back also gave me a little better understanding of things as a receiver as well. I was better able to understand what they were trying to do when they used their leverage and began to understand a little more where the weaknesses were in certain coverages. It wasn't like it helped me crack the code or anything, but it was insight I could use at my normal job.

After the Jets game, we had a *Monday Night Football* match-up with the Chiefs. I really felt like I was able to show my face again after that one. I was on the field for a dozen snaps in our dime (six defensive back) defense, covering their lightning-fast back Dexter McCluster, and we also had a seventy-two-yard punt return for a touchdown in a 34–3 win. I was so happy. It was a great team win against a conference opponent on a Monday night. I was happier than I'd been for a while.

Against the Eagles a week later, I actually blitzed Vince Young. I hit him square, but Vince was a large human and I messed up my back because he was so big. I also had an open-field tackle on him in the red zone and even thought I had a chance for a pick-6 when I was covering DeSean Jackson on a return route. My eyes got big but Vince saw me trying to undercut the route and threw it short and into the ground.

The next week, I was our nickel defender against the Redskins and was assigned to cover Santana Moss. I was out there trying to get under his skin because I knew what receivers hated. I'd hold him until he was five yards downfield and yank his jersey. He was getting pissed, saying, "I have a receiver on me, get me the ball!" We won that game on defense when Jerod Mayo picked off a Rex Grossman pass at our 5 with thirty seconds left. What a fun experience. My back was so sore that game I called to one of our trainers for a hot pack after every defensive series.

We rolled into the playoffs that year on an eight-game winning streak. We hadn't lost since the Giants game on November 6, and were the number one seed in the AFC with a 13-3 regular season record. In the divisional round, we beat Denver and Tim Tebow 45–10. That gave us a home game against the Ravens in the AFC Championship, with the winner going to Super Bowl XLVI in Indianapolis.

The year before, we'd been 14–2 and didn't get out of the first round. Now we were in against the Ravens, a hard-nosed team that we knew wasn't going to be intimidated. Especially not after they'd come into Foxborough two years earlier and beaten us so badly in the postseason. But we were a different team now. We'd turned over a lot of the roster since that day and were young. It was all about who would execute in a high-stress environment. It was a heavyweight fight for the right to get to Indy.

We got up on them early with a field goal from Stephen Gostkowski, but this was a game in which no team could get separation. It was 3–3, then 10–3; 10–3 and then 10–10. The Ravens finally pushed ahead in the third on a touchdown by Torrey Smith that made it 17–16. Smith broke loose from our corner Sterling Moore on that play and got down the sideline. On the next kickoff, Danny Woodhead had a nice return going but fumbled. Baltimore turned that into a Billy Cundiff field goal to make it 20–16 late in the third.

We got the ball back at our own 37. Plenty of time to go ahead, but on the first play of the drive, we took a blow. After a twenty-three-yard catch, Gronk injured his ankle, and it was clear his night was over. On the next play, Tom threw to me deep down the left sideline, but he was intercepted by Cary Williams. It was the second time in the game Tom was picked looking to me; the first was in the opening quarter when I ran a seam route and Lardarius Webb made a play inside me. Tom was hot after that one because anytime a defensive back is able to get inside a receiver and make a play on the ball, both the quarterback and receiver know the DB beat them. Fortunately, this time there was a flag on the play, so we had a reprieve. Tom wound up getting the touchdown to put us up 23–20, vaulting in from the 1 on a fourth-down play.

Now we had to hang on. And I was in the middle of it defensively because we were in dime coverage. I played twenty-two plays on offense and twenty-two on defense in that game, but the one I would remember for a long time was the one I screwed up. On a third-and-1 near midfield we had something called a "lock and combo" coverage called against their bunched receivers split to the left of their alignment. We had a miscommunication and Anquan Boldin, who was the inside receiver, looped outside. I stayed inside, and that left Boldin by himself. He gained twenty-nine yards down to our 23, putting the Ravens in field goal range. We were almost certainly going to overtime. Actually, we were almost going home.

After the Ravens failed to score, Billy Cundiff had just a thirty-two-yard attempt with fourteen seconds left to tie the game. Somehow, he hooked it. Badly. I couldn't believe it. I'd gone from helping the Ravens into field goal range with my blown coverage to suddenly realizing we were going to the Super Bowl.

Losing Gronk was a big blow, though, there was no getting around that. But our focus was on the Giants. We couldn't feel sorry for ourselves. He did his best to get ready for that one but it was clear he wasn't himself, and when the game came, he was definitely not himself.

Witnessing a Super Bowl firsthand for the first time was overwhelming. The crush of media, the same questions day after day, knowing the entire sports world was focused on that game and every angle of it was fun but surreal. The position I was in—part-time offense, part-time defense, full-time special teams—meant I was locked down on my assignments and on studying. The last thing I needed was to be in the spotlight for a mental error in the Super Bowl. The Giants spent the week talking about how much they wanted to see me out there covering Victor Cruz. Mario Manningham, one of the Giants' receivers, sent a message when he said to me through reporters, "This ain't your real position, we'll expose you." I didn't take the bait but it pissed me off, no doubt.

As it turned out, I wasn't involved much at all, on either side of the ball. I had three kickoff returns and wasn't out there on offense or defense. I didn't get an opportunity to help and honestly, I kind of blocked that game out. We lost 21–17 after being ahead 17–9 in the third quarter. It was so disappointing personally and for the team.

I went into that off-season with Coach Belichick's warning echoing in my ears: "You're at a crossroads."

That's me on the left, with Nicki and Jason. Do I look ready for some football?

Left and below: Here's a throwback to my running back days with the Redwood City Niners, the 1998 Pop Warner National Champions.

High school baseball. All I can say is baseball led to a lot of wild confrontations with Dad.

Late in high school I finally hit my growth spurt and people started noticing Woodside High's dual-threat quarterback.

My girlfriend and prom date Jaqui Rice. Her dad happened to be a guy named Jerry Rice, a player you may have heard of.

The Kent State Golden Flashes
gave me an opportunity to
bring the hard work ethic I
was raised with to a program
that had become accepting of
mediocrity, and the experience
helped me get to the NFL.

My first billboard!

Draft Day (2009) was an
emotional rollercoaster
with Mom and Dad that
ended with a call from
Bill Belichick and the
beginning of my career
with the New England
Patriots.

The day Lily Rose was born and my world changed.

Scott O'Brien taught me, a guy with no experience, kick returning and the importance of executing on special teams.

Chad O'Shea (left), our wide receiver coach, and Josh McDaniels, the brains behind our high-powered offense.

When Tom Brady (the G.O.A.T.) says something, you listen.
Our countless hours throwing, catching, running routes,
and training together continue to make me a better player.

Matt Slater, one of my best friends, has been there through
all the ups and downs.

Danny Amendola was already a good friend before he came to the Patriots in 2013. Since then, Dola has become like family.

With my agents Carter Chow, Don Yee, and Steve Dubin, who believed in me from the beginning.

Michael Zagaris/Contributor/Getty

Above and right: "The Catch." There was no way I was going to drop that ball.

Focus On Sport/Contributor/Getty

Al Bello/Staff/Getty

Tom Brady and me celebrating after Super Bowl LI. We've grown incredibly close and I'm lucky enough to call the old man a friend.

Winning the Super Bowl again proved Coach Belichick is a master of the game. His demanding style of coaching delivers greatness. Thanks Coach!

A NEW LEAF

If there's one constant in the NFL, it's change. Billy O'Brien, our offensive coordinator, left after the season to become the head coach at Penn State.

I'll always be grateful to Billy O. for how hard he was on me and the expectations he set. Nobody was more passionate than Billy, and when I messed up, he'd MF me to the moon and back, but I'll never forget the number of times after a bad practice when he'd come up and put his arm around me and say, "Hey, you know you have tomorrow, right?" I was happy for him to be moving on—that's the nature of the business— but I knew I'd miss hearing that Boston sarcasm coming out of him.

Billy O. was replaced by Josh McDaniels, who rejoined the staff during the playoffs. Josh had gone to the Saint Louis Rams as offensive coordinator after two seasons as the Broncos' head coach. When the Rams staff was let go after the 2011 season, he came back to New England, where he'd spent the first nine seasons of his NFL coaching career. Josh and I had no history together, as he'd become the Broncos' head coach the year I was drafted.

When free agency opened in 2012, there were more personnel changes. The Patriots signed Anthony Gonzalez, a former first-rounder from Ohio State, as well as Brandon Lloyd, who Josh coached in Saint Louis. They also brought back two fixtures from the 2007 Patriots: Donté Stallworth and Jabar Gaffney.

I didn't know what McDaniels would think of me. I was brand new to him, and my first thought was, *This guy is trying to get me out of here. He's trying to round up his boys, and I won't have a spot.* Any time there is a new coach, the players are a little uncomfortable. Everyone pays attention to who is getting reps and noticing when he's not in there. I needed to earn my reps with Josh, and, on top of that, after barely playing in the Super Bowl and being officially put on notice, I needed to prove myself again. My aim was to arrive in Foxborough and immediately show the coaching staff that I was in shape and that I'd been working harder than all the other guys.

That off-season, it wasn't just working out and catching balls at API, my workout spot in California; it was doing all that *and* running routes whenever I could. I threw that off-season with Carson Palmer, Matt Leinart, and Matt Cassel. Wes, who was coming off a monster 2011 season in which he had 122 catches for 1,569 yards in the regular season and another 18 catches in the playoffs, didn't go to LA that summer, so that meant Tom needed someone to throw to more often. I took advantage of the opportunity, running seventy routes with Tom up and down the field at UCLA. He ran me into the ground, and I could feel everything improving: my feet, my hands, my wind.

My day started at API around seven, when I'd do physical therapy and foam-roll my body out. Then I'd get on a bike for twenty minutes. Our group workout would begin around nine and last two hours. When that was done, I'd drive to USC or Manhattan Beach to throw with someone or go to UCLA to throw with Tom. I was all over LA that summer in the old Jeep Cherokee.

I lived with Ben Rawitz in Tom's house on Westridge Road in Brentwood. That house was about three miles from the massive estate Tom and Giselle built and moved into in 2012 (and sold in 2014 to Dr. Dre for $40 million). Tom had no idea I was living in his former house with Ben. Even though I don't think he would have minded, we hid it from him that I was there. Why risk it?

Ben is Tom's right-hand man and basically helps Tom manage his life. Being around both Ben and Tom that off-season helped me in so many ways, especially with eating better and being more consistent. In years past, I'd take three weeks off and run around with my high school buddies until the start of March. Not this year. Every morning, Ben would wake up and we'd have protein time—a big shake—and then we'd be on our way. It was impossible to eat bad living at Tom's house. We would raid the fridge and there wasn't one damn thing in that household that was bad for you.

Ben used to say that if Tom told me to be on the moon tomorrow morning with two footballs ready to throw, I'd be standing there in a space suit. I think Ben was impressed by that and it made him want to help me because he understood how much I wanted to succeed. He also wanted to make sure Tom had someone reliable to throw with, and I was becoming the most reliable guy in terms of being wherever he was. Tom needed that because he didn't always plan out his entire day down to the minute, so I needed to be on standby all the time.

I would train until my legs felt like jelly, pushing to the point of breaking five days straight, recover on Saturday and Sunday and then I would do it again. Each week, I felt myself getting quicker into my routes. I no longer had to think about the steps and the foot placement—I was truly becoming a receiver.

I mentioned how Dad told me I was ten thousand balls behind all the other receivers when I was drafted, so I'd have to work that much harder to make up the difference. I felt that sense of urgency again, and running routes for me that off-season was like getting ground balls from Dad five days a week. Your body learns habits and your mind makes sure the habits are correct. Pushing through the mental and physical exhaustion and still executing is when gains are made. I truly believe that.

With all the additional work with Tom, I felt we began to flow. He started to learn my body mechanics and I started to learn what he liked and didn't like. Finally we were doing those two-minute drills or sets of ten, and they were becoming easy for me. I wasn't dying or mentally frustrated, and I started to understand better what he wanted on certain routes. I wasn't hearing him yell quite as often after an incompletion where I cut too early for his liking, "You can't break it off like that!" I was gaining trust.

Meanwhile, the Patriots were negotiating a long-term deal with Wes, who was about to become a free agent. They didn't get it done before free agency began, so they put the franchise tag on him, which meant he'd make more than $9 million on a one-year deal. When the tag was put on, both the team and Wes seemed optimistic that they'd work out a new contract soon.

If they weren't able to, Wes would be a free agent after the 2012 season, and so would I. Wes was still the best in the business at that point, but I no longer viewed him as invincible. Each year, I had more experience under my belt, and during that off-season, even though I didn't have the reps or the production of Wes, for the first time I felt comfortable saying, "Hey, I can play this game, too."

I showed up to OTAs in really good shape—midseason shape. My goal was to turn heads the first day, and I did. Our strength coach, Harold Nash, noticed that I was in good condition and said it was obvious I'd been "working," and Coach Belichick was happy with my endurance. I'd put myself in the best position to atone for 2011.

The Patriots did come to me with an extension offer before the season. It was more money than I was currently making, but we decided I'd be better off addressing it after the season so we passed on it. I felt I was going to get a lot of time on the field in 2012 and I was confident in my ability to make plays and have the best season of my career. I didn't want to lock myself into something and think later that I should have bet on myself and gotten better value. It was encouraging, though, that the team indicated it wanted me around past 2012, especially with everyone it brought in during the off-season.

By the end of camp, I realized that worrying about the other players, making comparisons to Wes, none of it was productive. I had enough to worry about with myself, period. That's something that took time for me to learn. Control your day. Control you. You earn your role through your own practice and play, not someone else's. In earlier years, I'd bitch and pout over shit; now it was a "let's go compete and play some football" mind-set.

We had joint practices with the Saints in August leading into our preseason game. I was looking forward to it because, finally, the game was moving slower for me. I didn't have to think about the play when I lined up, I knew it cold. I knew the coaching point on the play. I knew the adjustment. How involved was the process on every play? Let me put it to you in the terms we use. If, say, it was single-high man coverage,

I was going to single release and burst in my vertical, burst to my depth, hit him at the top, and break in. If it was cover-5, I was going to attack like I was going inside, use my quickness to stack them, and then get them off at the top. I grasped those things. Once that happened, I could build in the way I ran a route.

I was also developing my own style. Previous to 2012, I stole from more experienced guys, such as Wes's jump cut. My body was bigger than his, so I could add to my moves by using my body on guys, using an elbow to create separation or use my lateral quickness against bigger guys. I was developing my own style of play.

Our home opener was week 2 against the Cardinals. I started this game instead of Wes and that caused a lot of conversation about whether Wes was being pushed aside. I understood why people would be interested in the conversation: Wes led the NFL in catches in 2011. He was playing under the franchise tag. He wasn't starting. It's a story. But whatever was going on there was not my concern. If I was in for the first play, the fifth play, the fifteenth play, my job was the same. And it would be the same for any other player.

Wes began the second drive on the sidelines as well but was on the field quickly after I was tripped up after catching a screen pass and landed on the back of Aaron Hernandez's ankle. I felt terrible because he was one of our stars and he was going to be sidelined for a month. Wes and I played together extensively for the first time, and we combined for ten catches and 145 yards. But we lost 20–18 and, as it usually is after a loss, the mood was anxious, tight as a violin string. We didn't play the way we should have played, and now it was on to Baltimore. Any conversations people wanted to have about Wes's role or my role were wiped away by preparing for the Ravens and Bill's message.

Bill keeps us from getting caught up in media stories simply by keeping us busy with a constant focus on football. The pressure is always on, so you don't have time to worry about what this or that means. If you don't do something right, there is a thing called the "lowlights." If you make a bad play, you'll be in the lowlights. No exceptions. Anyone feeling like they're playing pretty decently can expect to be on the lowlights. It's an inventive way for Bill to keep us all on edge and make sure our egos are in check.

Which brings us to the Ravens. Sunday night on NBC, a rematch of the AFC Championship. I had a big role in the offense for this one, and I was amped up. We opened the game with three tight ends; Brandon Lloyd was the only wide receiver on the field so there was no bullshit about whether I started instead of Wes. But I was involved plenty and the game was electric. Josh had me in for a couple of drive-starters and Tom looked for me twice on third down in the first quarter. In the second quarter, another injury hit me. I was blocking downfield for Danny Woodhead when I caught my hand in the shoulder pad of the Ravens' corner Jimmy Smith. It twisted around and by the time I got it loose I could feel it throbbing. I tried to pull my glove tighter, hoping it would pass, but it didn't. I definitely wasn't coming off the field, though. Not in that situation. We were moving the ball.

We finally got down to the Ravens' 7 with thirteen seconds left in the first half. Tom went to me on back-to-back plays. I scored on the second one, a little seven-yard touchdown when I split the defenders who were in zone coverage near the goal line.

Unfortunately, I had a broken hand, and once the trainers had a look at it during halftime and took an X-ray, I was done for the night. Injuries are the worst because not only are you not playing, someone else is getting an opportunity, and in the NFL, he's probably pretty good. That's reality. Everyone wants his team to do well and see other guys do well, but if you're not on the field, you're losing your opportunity. That's a fact. After being used more often on offense in a single game than I'd been since my rookie year, I was now going to the sidelines. And we lost 31–30. It was an all-around shitty night in Baltimore.

I was down for the next three games and saw only limited action in our matchup with the Jets on October 21. Next up, the Rams in London. I'd never been out of the country before, so that was an experience. And I loved London. I went out a few times by myself just sightseeing or with Rob Ninkovich or Matt Slater. Walking around Hyde Park, seeing Big Ben, Buckingham Palace, the London Eye was totally different for me and really gave me the travel bug. But for a game it's definitely a pain in the ass. I wound up jet-lagged, and if you've never been abroad—which a lot of NFL players haven't—it's a tough way to make your first trip to Europe. Routines are important in the NFL, and between the food and the travel, the trip messes with your routine. Both teams have to deal with it, so there's no disadvantage in the game, but it's not an ideal situation for the players.

We took care of the Rams in London, then blitzed Indy 59–24. Against the Colts I had a sixty-eight-yard punt return for a touchdown, a two-yard touchdown catch on a slant, and a forty-seven-yard run on a reverse that set up a Stevan Ridley touchdown. I finished the game with five catches for fifty-eight yards. I needed a game like that, and I started to get my feel back and return to the swing of things.

We had a short week after Indy because of the Thanksgiving-night game against the Jets. In the NFL, you don't really have the same Thanksgiving everyone else does, because the holiday falls right in the middle of game prep for

Sunday. If we weren't playing, I probably would have gone to Logan Mankins's house with a bunch of the fellas. As it was, we had a hard week of practice because we were playing in the AFC East against the Jets and, Rex being Rex, you knew he'd try to make things interesting.

After a scoreless first quarter, we unloaded on them in the second with thirty-five points. There was an eighty-three-yard touchdown to Shane Vereen on a wheel route; Steve Gregory had a fumble return-touchdown after the infamous "Butt Fumble" play when Mark Sanchez ran smack dab into his lineman's ass; and on the kickoff after that touchdown, Devin McCourty forced a fumble that I plucked from the air and returned for another score. Five minutes after that, Tom found me for a fifty-six-yard bomb after a blitz look the Jets gave us. I'd never really been a part of an explosion like that, and we were flying high.

Looking back, I almost feel like we let up a little bit. Or at least I did. And you can't let your guard down, because these are some of the best athletes in the world and they will hit you, ready or not. In the third quarter, I came from left to right and took a reverse toss from Tom. I had some room in front of me and thought I could split defenders and get into the clear. So I cut to my left, back toward the flow of the defense. You aren't supposed to cut back on a reverse. Too many people are coming. LaRon Landry reminded me why that's a thing. He hit me like a train and I fumbled before I hit the ground. Our helmets clashed on the play and I was done for the night.

There's a lot of focus on head injuries in the NFL now, and there should be. The dangers of repeated head trauma and the reality of chronic traumatic encephalopathy (CTE) is very real. But the risk is part of what we sign up for. We live an unbelievable life, and injuries, including head injuries, are a fact of NFL life. There is risk in all sports. It is what it is. I try to keep my body as well tuned and rested as I can. I know your head is not supposed to get bashed in repeatedly. I try to be as proactive as possible in the way I take care of myself. Technology is getting better, diagnostics are getting better, and I feel that we are well supervised. I am not going to bitch about what can potentially happen someday, because playing in the NFL has ultimately given me my dream, and my dream is to go out and play in Super Bowls and win Super Bowls doing a job I love.

After the win over New York, we had ten days off before we played at Miami. We were 8-3 at that point, and I felt like I was part of things in a way I hadn't been before. Offensively and on special teams, I was part of the plan every week. It felt like things were coming together.

And then I broke my foot. I was pushed when I was cutting and I bumped off Hernandez. I tried to put my foot in the ground and pivot and it snapped. I couldn't even walk on it. Our trainer, Jim Whalen, worked with me on the sideline and tested it. We went in for an X-ray, and I was still holding out hope it was a midfoot sprain, but the pictures showed a crack. Early in the next week, Coach Belichick called me into his office and told me I'd be put on injured reserve, ending my season. It wasn't a surprise but it was still a huge disappointment to know I was done for 2012.

That's the roller coaster of the NFL. I had two good games back-to-back, I had four touchdowns in two games—I wasn't accustomed to that—I was having fun, and it was over in a snap. My stress level went up immediately. My contract was up at the end of the season, so I wondered if the old contract offer might still be on the table. I wondered if they'd want me or if they would add more guys in the draft or free agency. More than anything, I wondered, "Why did this happen to me?"

Part of it may have been not listening to my body. I'd practiced hard that whole year, with no downtime in the off-season. I'd felt things in my feet, some soreness, and I hadn't really paid attention. I'd worn terrible cleats, the absolute lightest slippers you could wear. Usually, you want to wear light cleats because you want to be as fast as possible. But you don't want to sacrifice support and stability. In other words, the things I was doing that I thought would help me may have been hurting me. It's a balance.

I was living that season in Foxborough again with Matt Slater and one of our offensive linemen, Ryan Wendell. After the injury, I thank God I had Slater around me. Slates has been as big a part of my NFL success and my growth as a man as anyone. He is a positive guy, true at heart, and so giving. He's a devout Christian, and when he says he's praying for you, it's not just words. You know he's actively speaking to his higher power on your behalf. I've been with him through some of the lowest points in my life—the Halloween incident, the injuries—and he was the perfect person to help me and keep me mentally afloat.

Slates doesn't have to say anything to make an impact. Just the way he lives and conducts himself sets a standard. I was actually afraid to bring girls back to the house when Slates was there because I didn't want him to disapprove. I learned how to be a man and I truly strive to be like him.

That season went on without me. You're in a lonely place when you're hurt. You want to help but know you can't. You suddenly miss going to the team meetings you were complaining about a week earlier. Your team is the training staff and watching morning TV with them while rehabbing. You don't feel as much a part of what's going on, that's for sure. It's a big psychological battle. In 2012, I had really good camps, I was starting to play well, and then to have the hand and the foot? I just didn't know why I couldn't stay healthy.

In the playoffs, we got as far as the AFC Championship game, where Baltimore got its revenge for 2011 and won going away, 28–13. The season was officially over, as was my four-year rookie contract. On the one hand, getting to the end of that contract was an accomplishment. A converted quarterback taken in the seventh round who'd never played special teams, I survived four seasons with the best organization in the NFL, playing for a legendary ownership family and a Hall of Fame coach alongside some of the best players that ever played.

I made it through a broken forearm, a broken hand, and foot injuries my first two seasons, and I was now a free agent coming off a broken foot in 2012. After another great season, Wes was going to be a free agent. If he left, I was the heir apparent. How did the team view me?

A BREAKOUT SEASON

When it came time to negotiate the new contract, it was clear the Patriots did not value me the same way they had the previous summer. The two-year deal was now a one-year deal for $715,000. While I was processing that, Wes hit free agency. The Patriots didn't wait around to see whether they'd get a chance to re-sign Wes. They found a replacement right away. It was my training buddy Danny Amendola, brought in on a five-year, $28.5 million contract. The sudden turn of events stunned everyone. Wes had been a Patriot for six seasons and put up crazy numbers in 2011 and 2012. Now Wes was gone, joining Peyton Manning and the Broncos. The new Wes would be Dola.

It was a lot for me to process. My feelings were hurt, and I was mad with the thought that they had decided to move in a completely different direction. So I looked at other options. I visited the Giants and I had every intention of signing there. As far as the Patriots were concerned, I felt, *They don't want me. They don't need me. I'll go where I'm wanted.*

I met with the Giants' head coach, Tom Coughlin, the offensive coordinator Kevin Gilbride, and the wide receivers coach, Kevin M. Gilbride (the OC's son). The Giants reminded me of the Patriots. Coach Coughlin was similar to Coach Belichick in the way he talked about fundamentals and organization, which was no surprise since they had both been assistants on the great Giants teams of the 1980s. The vibe with the Giants was similar, too: family oriented but businesslike.

They were also similar to the Patriots in the overall value of their offer to me. A little more in signing bonus, but not enough to swing the decision. I spoke with Dad and my agents, and after a few days of thinking and talking, I realized a lot of it came down to Tom.

I'd been with him four years. I knew how he was with new guys and how hard it was to gain his trust. I was starting to have that trust. Understanding the system and Tom's likes and dislikes gave me a bit of an upper hand with the Patriots. The emotion of the decision was harder to handle than I expected. I remember talking to Ben Rawitz and being in tears as I sat on the couch discussing it. There were a lot of talks with Tom, and his message was, "Just trust me, Jules. Trust me. Just stay. I'll make it work." I put a bunch of trust into Tom.

I also felt that after a year under Coach McDaniels, I had an understanding of what he expected from me. It might change with Dola on the team, but I was still confident in my ability and my experience. I also realized that the position was probably going to go through a personnel overhaul and I was essentially the only receiver returning.

On the other hand, the Giants intrigued me. The drawback there was I would have been on the depth chart behind Victor Cruz, becoming more of a third-down guy and punt returner. I'd be proving myself and carving out space all over again.

Dad told me not to make decisions based on emotion. By the end of that first week of free agency, I had simmered down. Now my head and my gut said New England.

Decision made, I then had to address my right foot, which wasn't healing correctly. The technical term for the injury I suffered was a Jones fracture, which occurs on the outside of the foot. To stabilize the area and make sure the bone heals in proper alignment, a screw is inserted into the foot. It's not an uncommon injury in the NFL. Neither is the incidence of the area needing a second surgery, which I did. I probably pushed it too hard trying to prove how quickly I could recover and now my training was going to be affected all summer. I was concerned because somebody had to pick up the slack left by Wes, and I needed to be in that mix. How big a part of the offense was Wes? Tom threw to him 175 times in 2012 and 173 times in 2011. For comparison, Tampa's Mike Evans led the NFL in 2016 with 173 targets.

With Dola aboard it was obvious there would be competition between the two of us. But we'd been friends since we trained together during the lockout summer of 2011. Dola felt a little bad because he knew I was beat up about the whole situation with Wes leaving and how the team replaced him, but there were no hard feelings between Dola and me. It was business. Looking back at it now, I can see that I didn't have enough of a résumé for the Patriots to spend the money on me that they did on Danny. I missed sixteen games my first four years. I was hurt at the end of 2012. Danny had some really productive seasons with Saint Louis. Sometimes it's about timing and, unfortunately, my timing sucked.

The timing with my foot recovery wasn't much better. It stretched into training camp. Finally, Coach Belichick called me in and told me that the two rookie receivers they'd drafted, Aaron Dobson and Josh Boyce, were definitely making the team, so I needed to get out on the practice field ASAP. "We've got guys that are capable of playing," he said. "You've got to show me what you're capable of doing."

I wasn't 100 percent, but I knew I was out of time. Like my dad says, you can't snivel over it. And I understood Coach Belichick's perspective, too: He had a bunch of young receivers playing well. I was a guy who had been there four years but was having trouble staying on the field and had stuff to prove. Would I get the reps, or did the new guys get them? He had a decision to make.

I'd spent that off-season in a boot and riding around on a little gimp scooter, so I'd been off my feet for a long time. I had lost ground. But when Bill told me about the rookies, I felt like a cornered animal. I knew I had to fight my way out of it. My first few practices, I was sluggish. I had on new, heavier cleats, and there's a cautiousness you feel coming back from an injury in which your mind is involved more than it normally should be. I hadn't been running enough. Compared with 2012, when I never took a break, this was completely different. I'd been relatively idle.

But the way the previous year had gone, playing just nine games and having two injuries, I wondered if maybe I'd been too well conditioned. I'd redlined my body all off-season heading into 2012. Did working that hard and not getting enough recovery time cost me?

My first practice of 2013 training camp was at Philly for joint practices with the Eagles on August 6. I went down feeling off, not completely ready to compete, but after a few one-on-ones against the Eagles' defensive backs, sure enough, I felt it coming back. I was adjusting to the bigger cleats, and trusting that the foot was stable. All of a sudden, my confidence returned and it grew through camp. I was surprised. I won't say it was seamless, but with three rookies in the wide receiver mix—Dobson, Boyce, and Kenbrell Thompkins ("KT")—and Gronk still coming back from off-season back surgery and complications related to the broken arm, Dola and I were Tom's main targets.

There was another factor, too: the loss of Aaron Hernandez. His arrest and release is something I don't think anyone involved with the Patriots will ever forget. It was shocking and sad, a complete nightmare. In June 2013, Aaron was taken into custody at his home in North Attleboro for the murder of Odin Lloyd. Hernandez allegedly murdered Lloyd in an industrial park not far from his house. It was a terrible, terrible situation for everyone involved on all sides. You had Lloyd's family, Aaron's family (he and his fiancée had a little daughter) and it was just a lose-lose situation.

I don't know what was going down. It's pretty clear the guys involved weren't saints, but Aaron and I were friends only on the field. Aaron hung out with different people and had his own clique, so we didn't hang. I liked him and loved competing against him; he was so talented as a player and a really intelligent person. I still wish that he'd opened up to someone. But he kept to himself, and I got the feeling that's how he wanted it. Football life and away-from-football life. It was just a sad experience for everyone. Weird. The case was a big distraction.

A lot of guys didn't like Aaron because of the way he'd chirp on the practice field. He'd say some pretty aggressive stuff and people would laugh it off and say, "OK, Aaron." It wasn't just the things he would say; it was his attitude, too. Aaron was a very confident player, and that confidence—maybe a little cockiness—a lot of older guys didn't like, because he walked in with that attitude. But they couldn't really say much, either, because he was so freaking dominant on the field, but he definitely wasn't universally loved. Aaron was like a young buck looking to lock horns with the older bucks. That's kind of how Aaron was.

On the other end of the spectrum, we had Tim Tebow in camp competing as a quarterback. Tebowmania wasn't really a thing anymore. By 2013, Tim was coming off a tough season with the Jets and was looking for a chance. What a great dude he was. He worked hard, loved football, and took all the joking about his pure persona with a smile on his face. One time, when someone yelled, "Jesus Christ!" within earshot of Tim, he turned around, smiled, and said, "You know He loves you!" He was just a good guy to have around in the locker room. He didn't make it with us, but I love seeing him still at it, playing in the Mets organization.

With Gronk out, Wes in Denver, and Brandon Lloyd out of the NFL, Tom was running with completely new players. In 2012, 468 of his 637 attempts went to those three players and Hernandez. Now the only wide receivers with any depth of experience were Dola and me.

The season started pretty well for me and Dola. He played in the first game despite a groin injury before halftime. I knew he was tough before he got there, but he played the rest of the game hurt, catching 10 balls for 104 yards.

Having had groin issues my rookie year, I knew how hard it was to play receiver with that injury. Dola battled in that one. That day, the two of us combined for 17 catches and 183 yards, and I scored two touchdowns. When he arrived, Dola said that we were going to make each other better. He was right. It was a good team win for us, and after what I'd gone through with the foot and the contract in the off-season, it was a relief to get out of there with a win. I reminded myself not to get too excited. Last time I got excited, I got hurt.

Our second game was also in the division, a Thursday-night game against Rex and the Jets. I looked at the wide receiver personnel and thought, *I better take advantage of this.* In the past, opportunities I'd had didn't pan out because I was either injured or trying to do too much. This time, I stayed focused on the task at hand.

The game was a mess. It was played in a downpour and we were sloppy on offense. Tom threw to me on 18 of his 39 throws, and I had 13 catches for 82 yards—just about the worst yards-per-catch average in league history. We won, 13–10, but it was a struggle.

That was a tough stretch for everyone. It was really my first go-round at getting a lot of clock with the Patriots in my years there. Any transition in any facet of life is hard because you become comfortable with what you have. I'm sure Tom was comfortable with Welk and everyone else and he now had a whole new crop of guys. Tom had been in the same system for, at that time, fourteen years, and now he was dealing with guys starting fresh. There was frustration for everyone.

But anyone who knows us knows the beginning of the year is not when we're peaking, it's when we're developing our team. We were trying to improve every day, every practice, every meeting, every workout, trying to find out what we had to do to win ball games. As competitors, we felt that the frustration grew out of our high standards. Coach McDaniels likes to say, "Champions have championship standards, and championship standards don't know what time of year it is." So, regardless of whether it's OTAs, training camp, or the middle of the season, you still have to go out and get better that day. If you're not getting better, you're getting worse.

A couple of weeks later, we were back in prime time on Sunday night at Atlanta. The team was still trying to find its legs at that point but I felt like mine were under me. I'd been thrown into the fire after my second foot surgery and was doing whatever it took to keep my spot. Through the first three games, I had 27 catches. Now we were on *Sunday Night Football* on NBC, which had become the premier game of the week, like *Monday Night Football* used to be. Playing against an explosive team, we felt their dome rocking, and we measured up, winning 30–23. It was a fun game, and I had a couple of big catches and a career high in receiving yards (118), but there were still plenty of things I was getting MF'ed for, mainly the times I improvised to get open. When it worked and I caught the ball, nobody would notice that I'd mangled the entire construct and concept of the play. That's not team football, though, and our wide receivers coach, Chad O'Shea, told me a few times, "Hey, what are you doing? You can't do whatever you want to get open out there."

I hate to say it, but I learned that stuff from Welker. Sometimes it wasn't drawn up the way Welker did it, but when he got a twenty-yard gain on third down, no one was complaining. You can't do it too much, but being a football player, you sometimes have to make a play and you instinctively do something. But the coaches hate it because it just invites confusion.

Even after that win in Atlanta, our identity was still developing. The next week in Cincinnati we had a tough game on offense in the rain against the Bengals and didn't score a touchdown, losing 13–6. It was a repeat of the Jets game in week 2, only we weren't able to pull out a win. It was our first loss of the year, and we still needed to grow.

Two games from 2013 taught me a lot about football and what a team is capable of when it keeps its poise and plays a great situational game. There's no end to the time we spend on managing clock, time-outs, down and distance, and possessions, executing all the small things at key moments, which together exponentially raise the likelihood of winning. A team has to be ready when those key moments arrive.

Composure, confidence, and trust in your teammates are the key elements that allow you to execute. Coach Belichick believes those come with practicing situations as often as possible. There are times when you think, *Really? Are we going over this again?* When we won games in which we were all but dead, we understood why. We had three shining examples of that in 2013, the first of which was against New Orleans.

We played the Saints on October 13. It was a 4:25 p.m. start, and the Red Sox were playing the Detroit Tigers that night at Fenway Park in game 2 of the American League Championship Series. Boston gets electric when its teams are deep in the playoffs, and Gillette was wired that afternoon with both games on tap.

Dola was back for the first time since week 1, and we were up on New Orleans by halftime 17–7. We still led 23–17 late in the third, but the game turned with 3:35 left when Drew Brees hit Kenny Stills with a thirty-four-yard touchdown pass on a third-and-20. Suddenly, we were down 24–23. Coach Belichick rolled the dice when we got the ball back, going for it on fourth down from our own 24 with 2:50 left. We didn't pick it up and, after the Saints made a chip shot field goal to make it 27–23, we'd have to work the clock. That's what situational football is: understanding time, time-outs, down and distance, and playing the percentages. The answers aren't always obvious, and even though Coach Belichick makes the big decisions, players have to be tuned in to what the aims are. We spend an insane amount of time on situations during practice, and it pays off for us every season. Repeatedly.

We got the ball back with 2:24 left and Tom looked for me deep down the right side, but the Saints' corner Keenan Lewis came up with it. We looked cooked. We needed a stop on defense. We got it. The safety Steve Gregory came up with plays on first and second down, and then the Saints didn't really try to convert on third down and Chandler Jones dropped Brees for a five-yard loss. We took over at our own 30 with 1:13 left—then TB turned into TFB (that's Tom Fucking Brady).

Tom hit me up the seam for twenty-three yards to start the drive and get it out to the Saints' 47. I took a lick but held on. Then he found Austin Collie for fifteen, and Aaron Dobson made a nice catch on a fake-spike play and picked up six, struggling out of bounds to stop the clock with thirty-nine seconds left. Tom went for it all on the next two plays, throwing for me down the middle. The second one was right at the goal line and I just couldn't get my hands under it. Should have had it. Now it was fourth down, and Tom found Collie for nine. After spiking the ball to stop the clock with eleven seconds left, Tom dropped a seventeen-yard rainbow in to Kenbrell Thompkins for the game-winner. Amazing. And all because of situational football.

People ask what Tom is like when the pressure is on and we're hanging by a thread. He doesn't change much. He'll fire you up a little bit before we take the field for a drive and let everyone know the situation, but when the drive starts, he's more focused on the situation and what he wants. And he doesn't get all emotional when things go wrong. He's on to the next thing, immediately.

After Tom brought us back in the evening, David Ortiz did his thing that night at Fenway with an eighth-inning grand slam into the home bullpen as the Sox beat Detroit. Big Papi and TFB. Great bookends to a very good Sunday in New England.

We lost 30–27 in overtime the following week in New York on kind of a bullshit call that gave the Jets a second shot at a game-winning field goal. After games like that, I usually think, *I could have done better, I could have made that block, this catch.* Games like that come down to one play at the end that decides who wins and who loses. But you can't forget all the plays before the last play that put both teams in that do-or-die spot.

The Jets game also marked Gronk's first game back, and he made an instant impact. During the six-game span following the Falcons game, I wasn't getting the ball that often—I had eighteen catches compared with thirty-four in the first four games—but that's the nature of the beast in our offense. McDaniels doesn't design a game plan to "feed" any player, and Tom doesn't make decisions based on keeping guys happy. To play for the Patriots, you have to be selfless and understand that the coaching staff is doing what gives the team the best chance to win. Everybody wants the ball and everybody wants to make contributions. But in New England, the message is sent from the top down that asking "Where's mine?" or complaining about your role isn't viewed as wanting to win. It's viewed as a player thinking he knows better. Or being selfish. On a team with Bill Belichick, Tom Brady, and Josh McDaniels, you don't know better. So you shut up and trust the process.

I was still getting the ball plenty on returns, and the whole unit was doing a fantastic job. Through the first ten games, I averaged 11.5 yards on 26 returns. The returner gets credit on returns because he's the one with the ball, but it's all the guys in front of him doing their jobs that allow a returner to make any yards at all. I will never not love returning kicks, I don't care how old I get in this league. Special teams allowed me to play in this league while I was getting established. It allowed me to bring value. It takes passion, heart, and relentlessness. Some guys bitch and complain about being on special teams, but I love the reps and having the ball in my hands. I like trying to make something happen, and when everyone is doing his job on a return and it clicks, the euphoria that comes from those plays is second to none.

The 9-1 Broncos came to town for another *Sunday Night Football* game. Peyton Manning versus Tom Brady. Wes Welker's return to Foxborough.

I was fired-up for two reasons. Wes was a guy I'd watched up close for four seasons. At times he had been a mentor and someone who taught me a lot. I wanted to perform at a high level in front of him and show him I belonged. I also wanted to prove something to our team. I didn't want any second thoughts about my ability to replace Wes.

I know the way Wes left was difficult for him, and people in Boston took it hard. I have to admit, though, I didn't think about Wes's situation or how he felt about the Patriots when he left and signed with Denver. I was more worried about how I was going to get on the field and make the team. I wasn't "the guy" at the beginning of the season. I had a lot more to worry about than Wes Welker's emotions toward me or the Patriots. I needed to get my foot right and I was on a one-year deal, so there was a laundry list of stuff to occupy me other than that.

At kickoff, the temperature was 22 degrees, the winds were near 25 miles per hour, and the wind chill was 6 degrees. Perfect anti-Manning weather, right? Instead, it was 24–0 at the break. Over the howl of the wind we could hear boos from the chilled Gillette Stadium crowd as we headed to the locker room. I didn't blame them a bit. As with the Jets game, the Carolina game, and the Saints game, we couldn't play badly against teams and expect to stay in contact with them. We were doing it again. And it was embarrassing. Tom was losing his mind at the lack of execution.

We got the ball first in the second half and, going into the wind, put it in the end zone to make it 24–7. Denver loves to play press-man coverage, meaning their defensive backs will get their hands on receivers as we come off the line, then stick with the same receiver throughout the route. An offense counters that with routes in which receivers cross paths or loop around each other, creating traffic. To keep contact with their man, defenders have to either plow through receivers or go into a "trail" position where they're a step behind. On the touchdown, I lined up inside with Dola and Aaron Dobson out to my right. At the snap, they started upfield, and I crossed behind them. My defender, Quentin Jammer, got lost in the junk and Tom dropped a perfect throw to me over Jammer in the back right corner of the end zone.

We pulled to within three at the end of the third when Tom hit Gronk with a laser from the 6. Early in the fourth, Tom hit me in the right flat and I got a little squirrely on the cornerback Chris Harris, spinning out of his tackle, cutting to the middle, and diving into the end zone to make it 28–24.

A Stephen Gostkowski field goal made it 31–24, but you can't count Peyton out. Going into the wind, he engineered a touchdown drive to tie it and send it into overtime. That's when Coach Belichick made a gutsy call to take the wind in overtime and let Denver get the ball first and keep trying to drive into the wind. It was a stalemate in overtime until just three minutes were left. Wes was back deep to field a punt but Ryan Allen's boot came up short of where he was positioned. Wes decided to let it bounce, but one of Denver's blockers, Tony Carter, didn't hear Wes's shout to stay clear of the ball, and it bounced off his leg. We covered the loose ball and Gostkowski made a thirty-one-yarder—with the wind—for the win.

That kind of situational football and game management is just Bill being Bill. I never second-guess him, because he is right more often than he is wrong, that's for sure. We let him make the decisions, and it's my job to put the helmet on and try to make plays. I ended up with nine catches for 110 yards and two touchdowns in that Denver game, and in the next one—a win over the Texans down in Houston—I had nine for 103. But more important, it was a good team win for us. We followed up the Denver game going on the road and pulled one out.

The next game was another memorable comeback, but it came at a cost. We lost Gronk to an ACL injury when he was hit on the knee by the Cleveland safety T. J. Ward. That was a punch in the stomach. I've seen Gronk since his first year in the league battle and come back from injuries. It takes a psychological toll as much as a physical one, because coming back from an injury is such a long journey. It sucks when it is one of your buddies dealing with that shit, and you know that the only way he can be taken down is by going low on him. You see 220-, 240-pound guys bounce off him like flies, you understand why defenders do it. It's football. But you just hate to see that, and the Browns game got real chippy after that hit. There's a fine line between hard and dirty, and I think the percentage of guys in the NFL who are truly dirty and would try to injure someone is low. I know T. J. Ward. He's a friend of mine. I don't think he's a malicious player. I think he plays really, really hard, and it's a double-edged sword with Gronk and how you tackle him because of his size. The defender's job is to get him on the ground. It just sucks when an injury is the result of doing that.

We trailed 19–3 against Cleveland late in the third, and it was 26–14 with 2:43 left when we got the ball back at our own 18. Then came another dose of situational football. Shane Vereen and I had a couple of big receptions before Tom found me on the back line of the end zone for a two-yard score. I got blasted on the catch but held on, to make it 26–21. Then came the special teams. Gostkowski ran a perfect onside kick and we recovered it. Three plays and Tom found Dola for the touchdown. We escaped, 27–26.

Our coming back to win that game, as well as the ones against New Orleans and Denver, showed signs not only of brilliant coaching, but also of a tough team that knew how to execute. These were the games on my mind when we were down against the Falcons in Super Bowl XLI. If you've done it before, chances are you can do it again.

After a loss down in the heat of South Florida to the Dolphins, we went into Baltimore needing a win to give us a first-round bye in the playoffs and to prove to ourselves what kind of team we were heading to the postseason. We'd been dealing with injuries all season, and with Gronk down for the year, we had something to prove to ourselves.

We ended up with one of our best team wins I've been involved in. Slates had a huge game on special teams, the defense played great, with Chandler Jones and Tavon Wilson both getting defensive touchdowns, and LeGarrette Blount and Stevan Ridley had big days carrying the ball. We won 41–7 in Baltimore against one of our toughest rivals. That was a big one for us.

The final game of the regular season was at Gillette against the Bills. I went in with 96 catches and 991 yards receiving, but even more important to me personally was that I was playing in my sixteenth game. After all the injuries I'd been through in the past, all the worrying about my spot on the team and whether I'd stick around, to make it through the season without missing a game was a credit to not just me but to our training staff, led by Jim Whalen, our strength coaches, Harold Nash and Moses Cabrera and Alex Guerrero, who'd taught me so much about training and nutrition.

In a driving rainstorm, we beat the Bills 34–20. I caught nine balls for 65 yards to finish the year with 105 catches and

1,056 yards. You never want to think of individual stats as that important, you just want to go out and get a win; that's ultimately the best stat. But getting over 100 and 1,000 was a cool accomplishment.

One thing about that season was the number of guys who stepped up. Defensively, we had guys like Devin McCourty coming into his own as a top-tier safety. Dont'a Hightower and Chandler Jones, two first-round picks in 2012, really matured. Rookies like Logan Ryan and Duron Harmon in the secondary made big contributions. And Jamie Collins, another rookie who we took in the second round, really opened eyes.

Jerod Mayo was one of our defensive leaders and a captain. When he went down against the Saints with a torn pec, all the linebackers had to step up. Jamie certainly did. That kid is by far one of the best athletes I have ever seen in my life. He was just a down-south dude, mean as a two-headed rattlesnake, and that's what you want in your linebackers. When he's on the field, he doesn't like anybody. He improvised at times, but sometimes great athletes believe that there are things they can do that the scheme doesn't understand. Jamie was that kind of athlete. He was amazing. When we played Denver, we had him split out covering Welker on a few plays and he stuck with him. At 260 pounds.

After we beat Indy in the divisional playoff round, we went to Denver with a trip to the Super Bowl again on the line. It was our third straight trip to the AFC Championship, and it would mean another week of Brady versus Manning hype and revisitations of the decision to let Wes go to free agency.

That was a very good Broncos team. They'd gone 13–3 in the regular season and Peyton had thrown for a record 55 touchdowns. DeMaryius Thomas and Eric Decker both had well over 1,000 yards receiving, Wes had 73 catches, and their tight end Julius Thomas had 78. On defense, Von Miller was becoming Von Miller, and they had fast linebackers like Danny Trevathan and Wesley Woodyard. When the sun came up on January 19, it was a beautiful day, 65 degrees and not a cloud in the sky. We liked playing in the cold, and snow, and rain. We felt like that gave us an upper hand. There was none of that. It was a perfect day for throwing.

Denver got a field goal in the first, and then, early in the second quarter, there was a controversial play in which the Broncos ran a crossing route and Aqib Talib—who was covering Thomas—collided with Wes on a pick play. It was a hard collision, and we lost Aqib for the rest of the game. Coach Belichick was livid about it, and we all were disappointed to lose Aqib. He was one of our best defensive players. It was a game-changer.

Personally, I never get mad about that stuff. It sucks to have one of our best players go down, but this is not a nice sport. We're modern-day gladiators and we're trying to rip each other's heads off. You know there is going to be something like that going down. It's chaos out there when your season is on the line. One game from the Super Bowl, guys are laying it on the line. I tell younger players that the season gets more intense at every level. OTAs and training camp is like being in diapers, preseason games get faster, regular season games get even faster, and then in the postseason, this is what guys play for. They can see their goal. There is no next week. That is the show. Nothing comes close to postseason football in terms of physicality when people are after their Super Bowl rings. It's do or die, not a best-of-seven series. You win or you're on the couch the next week, planning golf trips.

That game was a case of a Broncos team that was hitting its peak while we fought to keep up. We didn't make any plays and the well ran dry. We lost 26–16. For the second year in a row, we were a game short of the Super Bowl. As I peeled off my tape in the visitors' locker room at Invesco Field, I pondered my football future. With my one-year deal up, I was facing another uncertain off-season. This, time, though, I had at least one season of solid statistics under my belt. So much of free agency and how well you do financially in the NFL has to do with timing.

Two months later, I was in the office of the San Francisco 49ers' coach, Jim Harbaugh. He asked, "What is it going to take to get you in a 49ers jersey?"

FIFTEEN

DESTINATION ARIZONA

When the Niners reached out to my agents, I was excited to take the trip to my hometown team. Detroit was also showing interest, and the Patriots, meanwhile, wanted us to keep them up on anything that was being considered. I sat in the Niners' facility breaking down film with their coaches, and Jim Harbaugh was an awesome dude. He was direct, funny, and he was all about football and competing. We definitely had a similar approach to the game in that it was all-consuming. We had mutual friends, I was from the area, and it was cool to think I could be a 49er, just like back in Redwood City. The Niners were hot back then; they had lost to the Ravens in the 2012 Super Bowl and lost to the Seahawks in the 2013 NFC Championship.

As I studied their offense, though, I didn't like the fit of what I would be doing. The Patriots were all about precision, whereas with Colin Kaepernick at quarterback, the Niners were more about freelancing and freeflowing on offense. It wasn't as calculated. I'm not trying to bring anyone down saying that, it was just something I wasn't used to. At one point, Harbaugh said, "How much are you looking for?" I told him that three years and $15 million with $10 million guaranteed would be nice. He said, "I think we could do something like that. Just don't tell my GM [Trent Baalke], because he'd kill me for talking numbers with you." I sat there thinking, *Oh my God . . .* I was a seventh-round pick who played out his rookie deal and then signed a one-year deal for the vet minimum. This was life-changing. As I was about to board a plane to Los Angeles, Don Yee called. New England had brought its offer up a significant amount and— best of all—it was real money. Some deals are announced and there are so many incentives a player has to reach, the numbers aren't real. The Patriots' offer of four years and $19 million was legit. I'd make close to $15 million in salary, signing bonus, and roster bonuses. And I'd get additional bonuses for every game I was on the forty-six-man roster. But Don said the Patriots wanted to know by the end of the day what I was going to do or they'd pull the offer. My brain started racing a little but Don, as he always does, centered me by being logical and calm. I decided I was comfortable with the offer so, right there, before I boarded the plane in San Francisco, I decided to stay in New England.

My agents did a great job, as usual. They aren't flashy guys and they don't seek attention. What they are, are guys you can trust and guys who are going to look at your situation from every possible angle and advise you to do what's best for you. That might not always mean going for the most money.

I could have taken more visits and drawn things out, but I thought, *Why? I'm comfortable here. I love the Patriots and the winning environment, I don't have to worry about the coach getting fired, and I won't have to start over.* I'd been in Boston five years. I loved the Celtics, the Red Sox, and the Bruins. I loved the Cape and being around the city. I just loved the life out there. It had become part of who I was, so I said, "Fuck it. I'm staying a Patriot."

The new contract led to an interesting realization for me. Before, I was trying to prove people wrong about me, trying to prove that I could go from quarterback to wide receiver and succeed in the NFL. Now I wanted to prove my coaches right. They believed in me enough to sign me up again. I battle for my coaches, the men who are ultimately the surrogate fathers and who provide the structure and authority that Pops used to provide. They are always the boss. Now it was like I wanted to go out and make them proud. I wanted them to feel like they did the right thing. Even with a new contract, it's understood that you don't automatically have your role. You go out and earn it every year. That's not an exaggeration. Look at 2012. Wes was franchised and making $9 million but I had a great off-season and saw my playing time increase. You have to "establish your level of performance" every season as our coaches like to say.

I threw with Tom a lot that off-season. After a good season, we were more comfortable with each other. The more you play with someone, that's how it goes.

Tom Brady

When Jules first got to the team, he was trying to find a role. We didn't really know what that role would be. It was a very challenging transition. He had a great skill set when the ball was in his hands, and early in his career we got the ball to him in easy ways. We'd run a reverse with him or throw him a screen so the ball would immediately be in his hands. As he developed as a receiver, he realized he had to work to get the ball. It was an evolution for him to do that. It takes a while. It takes trial and error. But a great advantage he had was playing quarterback, and he knew how to gain trust. And trust isn't action, it's more a feeling.

Jules was so committed to doing the right thing. I would ask him to be somewhere, and he'd be there early. He would never say no. When you see someone who's willing to commit, at this level, that really excites you. I've been around other players and that wasn't really their priority. I didn't know he moved to LA after his rookie year just to be near me in case I needed him—I wasn't trying to dis him. It was great to hear that, and it's a great lesson for other people to hear. You have to commit and be willing to change your routine. Whenever I called him, he was ready to go. Those sessions developed trust not only on the field but also off the field, and that still carries over today. He's someone I can always believe in. Jules in 2012 and 2013 was turning into a different kind of player than Wes. I don't like rating guys. Julian gets the highest compliments from me, and I can only give Wes the highest compliments, the same as Randy and Troy. They all posed different problems for a defense. Jules was really coming into his own while Wes was still just so good. People saw Julian as the next Wes, but he was really a different player in terms of size, speed, and the natural receiving skills that a guy has coming out of college. What you've seen since 2013 is an outgrowth of the work he put in the first few years. Unless you see the day-to-day, you don't really see what he's all about. He lives, sleeps, and dreams football.

Throwing with Tom was different from throwing with anybody else. When I throw with Tom, we start with some band warm-ups to get our bodies going. Then we do two-minute drills down the length of the field. He will call out a play and I will go out and run it. I will jog back to the spot and we do the next play. Once we get to the end zone, I'll be dead tired because it's nonstop. When I throw with other guys, it's different. It's more technical. It's a lot harder with Brady who's not only getting me tired physically because of the nonstop, no-huddle mentality, but he also makes me think, by saying I'm the "F receiver" on this play. It's taken hundreds of workouts but I've gotten to the point where I can do it and feel I've done it correctly. It's mentally draining when you have someone yelling at you, too. There would be times when I'd be dead tired and we'd be in the red zone and we would score then he would say, "Flag. Holding. We have to do it again." He always pushed me mentally. There were times when we would get up to sixty or seventy routes, though most of the time it's about forty-five to fifty routes.

Sometimes Alex Guerrero or Tom's buddy Kevin Brady (no relation to Tom) would join. We'd run the same play four different times with different leverage or technique each time. It was a way for us to get on the same page.

We added some players heading into the 2014 season who would make a big difference. On offense, the receiver Brandon LaFell (who everyone calls JoJo) was a big, tough, veteran guy who brought a presence to us. On defense, we added Darrelle Revis and Brandon Browner, and those guys made me better every day in practice. Going against Revis, you better not screw up anything. He was too smart. He knew everything a receiver could possibly try, and if you weren't disciplined, he would eat you up. And Browner, he was just so physical. If you didn't get off the line of scrimmage against him, you were out of the route.

Another guy that made us better that off-season was Malcolm Butler. Undrafted from West Alabama, he made the team on a tryout in June. He was so strong and so quick, I remember saying, "I thought this kid was undrafted from D2? Where did he really come from?!" While most defensive backs slow down when they turn back to look for the ball, Malcolm could speed up and never lose his bearings on where the receiver was.

These guys brought a different attitude to the team, for sure. With Revis, it was cool professionalism. Browner was pure, overpowering muscle. Malcolm was like the nastiest little dog you'd ever seen.

We also added a quarterback in second round of the draft that year, Jimmy Garoppolo. There was conversation outside the team about what this meant for Tom going forward and whether Jimmy was brought in to be his successor. I don't know if Tom saw it as a challenge—he's a very self-motivated person—but Bill and Nick Caserio, our head personnel man, do what's best for the team. I wasn't listening to the "Why did they bring in another QB?" shit. Every team in the NFL is going to lose players and add players. There is always going to be turnover. That is just the way the NFL works. The more you worry about other people and other stupid stuff going on, the more time you waste on your preparation and what you could be doing to make yourself better.

It was the same way when we traded Logan Mankins just before the 2014 season started. You knew it was a decision made above your pay grade. That didn't make saying good-bye to Mankins any easier. He had been in New England for nine seasons, been selected to seven Pro Bowls, and was a six-time All-Pro. You look at it and say, "Man, this is a crazy business." Logan Mankins, he was the War Daddy. No one brought it like Logan, and he barely said a word. He didn't have to. Tenacity just came off him, and you would see him week in and week out handle some of the strongest men in the NFL. He was the enforcer of our offensive line, and that was one of the things I worried when we traded him: *Who is our guy now? Who is our War Daddy?*

He brought his helmet and lunch pail to work every day and didn't say shit except a joke every once in a while. I loved him. I used to go to his house every year for Thanksgiving with him, his wife, Kara, and his little awesome kids; they are great people. It was definitely very tough to see him leave. Then, after we won the whole thing, I thought of a guy like Logan who never got the ring. That's tough.

You make some amazing friendships through football. You are around these guys more than you are around your own family. Fourteen-hour days, lots of traveling, and seeing each other at your highs and lows. I've developed a lot of relationships: Matthew Slater, Rob Ninkovich, Mankins, Nate Solder, Bryan Stork, Dola, Steve Gostkowski, Randy, when he was there. The friendships are a big part of it. Earlier in my career, the locker room wasn't as tight as it became from 2014 through 2016.

The organization has done a really good job of bringing in good team and good locker room guys. It has a huge impact on the feeling of a family type of atmosphere. It's not friendship. It becomes family. I literally love Matthew Slater like a brother. When you work hard with someone and you see what he is about and how he works, you bond with him. You feel a real synergy. Everyone has a story, with a different upbringing than yours, and they all come from different socioeconomic backgrounds. Black guys from the South, country dudes from the Midwest, city guys from New York and New Jersey. You learn these things about them and you can't help but be impressed. Everyone has a story of how he got to where we all are.

On the field, our regular season didn't start out well down in the heat of South Florida. The Dolphins just outplayed us in a 34–20 loss, and losing the opener in our division was like suffering a two-game swing. But it goes back to what I was explaining about 2013: it takes time to figure things out. It just so happened that in 2014, it took us some time to get our heads screwed on right.

We won at Minnesota in week 2, then won a sloppy one against the Raiders. There's a saying that "you'll always take an ugly win over a pretty loss" and that's true. We weren't playing up to our capabilities, though, and one thing I've learned over the years is that each and every team is going to give us its best shot. You can't let your guard down at all, or you're going to get knocked out.

Week 4 we got knocked out in Arrowhead Stadium by the Chiefs on *Monday Night Football*, 41–14. We usually do a good job of "ignoring the noise," as Coach Belichick calls it, but we heard the reviews after that game. On ESPN, Trent Dilfer said we were a weak team and added, "Let's face it, the Patriots aren't good anymore." My reaction? The season is not a sprint. It's a fucking marathon. It doesn't matter what you do at the beginning of the season. The real football season doesn't start until Thanksgiving. You have to put yourself in a position to compete, don't get me wrong. You need to win games. Every game is important in the NFL, because there are only sixteen of them. But we were still trying to figure out what we were about.

We knew we weren't playing well and we knew that we had to turn the page and improve, starting with a good week of practice. Ultimately that's where it all comes from. It's like painting a wall. You have holes in the wall? You have to spackle them, sand it, and prime it. The painting is the easiest part. It's the preparation to get the surface ready to go that's always the toughest. How does the wall look when you're all done? How well did you prepare it? That's a Frank Edelman special.

I don't remember any team-wide discussion of what Dilfer or anyone else in the media said, but we were all aware of what the perception was that week. Fuel.

Just six nights later, we were back in prime time and at home to play the Bengals, a team we failed to score a touchdown against in a 13–6 loss in 2013. We had an amazing week of practice that week. I don't know if it had to do with the loss to Kansas City, the way we lost, or the fallout after, but we were on point all week. On our first drive we served notice of what our 2014 team was going to be about from there on out. On the first play of the game, Tom hit JoJo for twenty yards, Stevan Ridley ripped off runs of nine and seven yards, Tim Wright—a tight end acquired when we traded Mankins—caught a thirty-yarder from Tom, and then TB ran for six. When we were at the Bengals' 5, we faced a fourth-and-1. Tom—who people had been speculating all week was in decline—muscled ahead for four yards and the first down. We beat the Bengals 43–17.

We then beat the Bills, Jets, and Bears, and we were clicking. We got punched in the face early in the season and then our mental toughness developed. When I look back on 2014 and compare it with 2016, I can see that both seasons had very real challenges for us at the start that helped us bank some belief in ourselves that would serve us well later on.

In early November, we had another *Sunday Night Football* matchup with Denver. This one didn't have the fireworks and drama of our 2013 regular-season matchup. We scored 24 in the second quarter and went into the break up 27–7 on our way to a 43–21 win. I had two touchdowns in the big second quarter, the second one on an eighty-four-yard punt return. After I scored and returned to the bench, I realized that Brady was in the end zone with me. I wanted to make sure it was him, so I asked him if he ran onto the field. "Yeah," he said. "I had to go see my guy!"

That's something we all love about Tom; he is absolutely one of the boys. He'll crack his joke here and there. He may be forty years older than everyone but he does things to try to keep himself young and hip. We just have to remind him sometimes that it's not 1982 anymore!

After our bye we went to Indy and put it on them again. As we had in the playoffs the year before, we outmuscled them and imposed our will. Jonas Gray ran for 201 yards and four touchdowns, and we had 246 yards on the ground. When a team just can't handle you like the Colts couldn't handle us, it must lead to the level of desperation that we'd see from them later in the season.

I got dinged at Indy when I smashed into a down marker and wound up with a deep thigh bruise, but the training staff and Alex Guerrero did a terrific job getting me ready for Detroit, where I had one of my busiest games of the year. I caught 10 passes on 15 targets and actually brought a punt back seventy-four yards for a score, but it got wiped out by a hold. That was a really fun game, and one thing that stood out to all of us was the way our defense and secondary were playing. We were in a stretch where we were playing another outstanding quarterback every week—Jay Cutler, Peyton Manning, Andrew Luck, and Matt Stafford—and the defense was stepping up every week. What we were seeing in practice from that group, other teams were starting to see on Sundays.

As a team, we were really gaining momentum. We needed that, because we were facing a challenge on the road against the Packers and Aaron Rodgers and then San Diego.

Most of us had never played at Lambeau Field before, so visiting Green Bay was a cool experience. It's probably what it feels like for a baseball player when he plays at Fenway or Wrigley for the first time—you just feel the history in the place. We didn't play our best in that one on either side of the football and lost 26–21 but it was a battle between two really good teams and a nice checkpoint for us to tell us once again what we were all about. We learned more about ourselves in the following days: Instead of heading back to New England after the game at Green Bay, we flew to San Diego to spend the week preparing for the Chargers on the West Coast.

Travel is a challenge in the NFL, and a lot goes on behind the scenes to get a team of fifty-three players, practice squad guys, coaches, front-office personnel, and support staff situated on the opposite coast for a week. I really don't know how they do it, so hats off to all those people. The team grew that week. We visited the Naval Medical Center in San Diego, a visit set up by our team medical director, Matt Provencher, who was chief of sports medicine at Mass General. Dr. Provencher worked with navy Special Forces and SEAL teams, and Coach Belichick, of course, has a long history with the Naval Academy because his father, Steve Belichick, was a coaching legend at Annapolis. The visits we make with wounded veterans or children around Boston on a regular basis were some of the highlights of my time in New England. I truly believe we get more out of those visits than the people we are supposed to be cheering up and encouraging, and the same was true in San Diego. It's a very, very humbling activity, and I think the Kraft family and Coach Belichick deserve an amazing amount of credit for always stressing the importance of being out in the community for volunteer work.

We were banged up going into San Diego. Defensively, both Chandler Jones and Dont'a Hightower were dealing with tough injuries, and I'd suffered a deep bruise on my other thigh against the Packers, so now I had matching bruises. That's a fact of life in the NFL. The injury rate is 100 percent. Every team has injuries every single week. Being able to deal with them psychologically and not make excuses about who's missing is something we're trained for, and I think we've done an excellent job of that over the seasons I've been with the Patriots.

We got a win in San Diego against a pretty tough team, and that showed a lot, bouncing back after the loss in Green Bay and staying in a hotel all week. It was a real turning point in our season, and one of the things I remember about that game was the fan support we had in the stands in San Diego. You can hear them wherever we go, and believe me, it's a huge lift having fans in enemy territory.

After that game, guys seemed to really lock in. We knew we had a special season going at 10–3 but it was important for us to stay in the moment, week by week, and keep on doing what we were doing. Just try for improvement in practice and stay on task.

Locking in means that sometimes you seal yourself off. I call my parents after every game to let them know I'm all right, and Dad will give me his spiel on what he thinks I should have done better, the old Frank Edelman coming out. I try to call my brother, Jason, once a week. But it's tough when you are in the grind; you don't always make the time.

Sometimes I just don't feel like talking to anyone. Doing what we do, everyone always wants to talk football with us.

Don't get me wrong, I understand and try to be cool with everyone because people love debating and discussing the game, but it can wear on me sometimes. I arrive at the facility super early and I leave late; my body hurts; I'm trying to recover form the week before and prepare for the next game. I'm lucky my parents understand that I don't always want to talk and they will give me my space. Dad lets everyone know, "Hey, he's fucking working, give him space." He understands that it's work.

Against the Dolphins the following week, we won pretty easily, 41–13. Unfortunately, late in the third quarter I took a hit and ended up leaving the game with a concussion. I spent that week in the concussion protocol, and between that and the two thigh bruises, Coach Belichick and the medical staff decided the best move was for me to take a couple of weeks off and get ready for the postseason. Part of me was disappointed, because I had 92 catches and it would have been an accomplishment to get 100 two years in a row, but you have to do the smart thing, and that was the smarter thing.

As the number one seed, we had a first-week bye and then met our old friends the Ravens. They'd won a very physical game on the road in Pittsburgh, 30–17. It was a cold one; 20 degrees with a wind that made it feel like 8 degrees by kick-off on Saturday night, January 10, 2015. I hadn't played in nearly a month. and for me, the layoff was tough. I like practicing, and I'm conditioned to the tempo of the season, so I had butterflies before the game. I knew that any game against Baltimore would come down to execution and finishing.

In the early stages, we didn't. The Ravens scored on their first drive, we were forced to punt, then they scored again to put us down 14–0. There was no panic. It was still early. We just had to get some first downs and stay smart situationally.

I remember Tom thought I was getting worked up, so he patted me on the back on the sidelines and told me to stay positive. We just had to get our shit right.

On the next drive, things got scrappy. Tom was sacked by the Ravens' Timmy Jernigan, who shoved Tom in the face. TB got angry. And defenses usually don't like it when Tom gets angry. He hit Gronk down the seam for forty-six yards—man, it was good to have a healthy Gronk for those playoffs—and capped the drive with a four-yard touchdown run.

By the time there was 10:22 left in the third, they were ahead 28–14. Plenty of time, but we needed to put the Ravens on their heels. That team had some veterans on defense—Terrell Suggs, Ed Reed, Haloti Ngata—and they play physically and with emotion. They were flying around at that point, so we slowed them down on the next drive.

We'd been practicing a formation trick during the year in which we would put a tight end at the left tackle spot and then split out a running back and put him on the line of scrimmage and make him ineligible to go out for a pass. Every time we ran it against our scout team, they'd get all messed up, so McDaniels, Belichick and Ernie Adams—a football genius who's known Coach Belichick since they were in prep school together dreams up things like this—knew they'd have an opportunity. We just needed the right time, and it was now.

We lined up Michael Hoomanawanui, a tight end, at left tackle and split out our running back Shane Vereen to the right but declared him ineligible. It worked. We picked up sixteen yards. We ran it again and went to Gronk for nine. Then, in their confusion, they got caught with too many men on the field and took a five-yard penalty. Tom then hit Hooman for another fourteen, and the Ravens' coach, John Harbaugh, took a fifteen-yard unsportsmanlike conduct penalty for coming onto the field. The Ravens kept covering Shane and leaving

Hooman open. Even after the referee Bill Vinovich specifically said on the stadium mic before a play, "Don't cover 34," they still covered him. That's not our problem.

The Ravens were pissed because they thought it was either an illegal formation or, at the very least, they should get a chance to match our personnel with substitutions. But Ernie knows the rules, believe that. I was more worried about my assignment. Tom finished the chaos-aided drive with a bullet to Gronk, and it was 28–21. Just as important, the Ravens were reeling a little. So we hit them again after Joe Flacco and their offense went three-and-out.

We opened the next drive at our 30. I caught a pass in the middle for nine, Shane caught one for ten. It was first-and-10 at our 49 with 4:28 left in the third. I'd gotten raked on my catch so I was still a little tired. Tom looked at me in the huddle and said, "We got the double pass."

The plan was for me to go in motion, step back after the snap, making sure I stayed behind Tom, who'd throw me a long lateral that would appear to be a screen pass, but I would then look for an open Dola downfield.

When Tom told me it was go time, Danny looked at me and gave this dramatic head nod. I'll never forget that. McDaniels had asked me whether I needed any notice before he called the play and I told him I didn't. Calling it in the middle of a drive off of a normal play didn't give me time to think about it, which was a smart move on his part. But I did think of the movie *Little Giants* and the trick play they ran, and I couldn't help but think, *Time to run "The Annexation of Puerto Rico."*

I did have nerves when I realized I'd be throwing. *I better not fuck this up if he's wide open.* At the snap, I made sure to get well behind the line of scrimmage, then, when Tom's pass hit my hands, I flipped it, got the seams, and saw that Danny was behind everybody. The coverage we were looking for was cover-4. That means four defenders lined up flat across the back of the defense, spaced out to cover the whole field.

Sometimes, a cover-4 defender on the outside will trap, meaning that corner will come up fast to support against the run or on little screen passes like the one we appeared to be running. If he bites, the safety to his left will have to get all the way to the sideline if it's not a screen. Really, all you need to do is have that corner bite a little, and that's what the Ravens' corner Rashaan Melvin did. The play design also had Gronk right in front of me, getting ready to block so the safety Will Hill came up to take on Gronk's block. Baltimore left the entire back side of the secondary unoccupied—except for Dola, who ran into the clear. For a second, I thought I'd overthrown it, but Danny ran right under it and, son of a gun, we got it. Gronk picked me up like a little kid and I started windmilling my arm to show I was loose. That saying that even a blind squirrel finds a nut? That was my day to be the blind squirrel.

That tied things up at 28, and we would go on to win 35–31. Meanwhile, in the other AFC divisional playoff on Sunday, the Colts knocked off Denver. That meant we'd see Indy for the third time in a little more than a year. The way we beat them in week 11, 42–20, and the way we beat them the previous year in the playoffs had to leave them feeling a little desperate.

We felt confident. We didn't underestimate them, but we knew we could carry out our game plan. We didn't want a repeat of the Ravens game, in which we were digging out of a hole all night. We had a great week of practice. We went in wanting to run the ball well, and we did that. We wanted to set up our play actions and did that. It was a blowout, 43–22. Honestly, when they go like that, you don't even remember those games. But we would remember this one, and not because of anything that happened on the field.

Days before the game, the Colts' GM, Ryan Grigson, emailed the league asking it to be on alert about the pressure of the footballs, because he believed we let air out of the balls after game officials inspected them. Why they would concern themselves with that a few days before the AFC Championship, when they should have been preparing for the game, I don't know. But that was the deal. None of us knew anything about all the stuff going on behind the scenes and nobody took it seriously when we heard about footballs being under-inflated the next day.

What do I know about a quarterback and his balls? I just catch them. I thought the whole thing was bullshit, to tell you the truth, the way Indy went about it. How many crazy cases of supposed football tampering had there been in the league? The Chargers had a towel covered with stickum that they didn't turn over in 2012. The Panthers and Vikings were heating up balls on the sidelines during the 2014 season. I don't even care about those things; all I know is that other teams did stupid shit like that in plain view of the officials and nothing happened. In our case, there was actually a scientific explanation for why the balls had less air pressure at halftime than when the game began. But the NFL, meanwhile, wanted to drop an A-bomb on us and try to ruin our quarterback's legacy over that stuff. It is what it is. That's my opinion on it. It sure looked like a witch hunt. There weren't any witches, though. The only reason we were different from any other team is because we won consistently. Period.

As it kept going and turned into so-called Deflategate, I just kept thinking, *Are we really talking about this?* The world was going crazy over a pound of pressure; meanwhile, my dad was a mechanic and he was telling me, "Yeah, when it's cold, things with air in them lose pressure." Pops solved it right away. But it just kept growing as the week went on. We were going to Arizona to play the defending Super Bowl champions and Tom's out there giving press conferences with no real information about what the NFL even found. It could have been handled differently, to say the least.

Despite what was going on, we were on to the Seahawks. I'd been to one Super Bowl, after the 2011 season, and I was not going to let the distractions get in the way.

SIXTEEN

YOU GOTTA BELIEVE!

We had eight days in Foxborough before heading to Phoenix for Super Bowl week, and we took great advantage of it. Even with the perceived distractions swirling, we were locked in, especially when we held a blue-and-white intrasquad scrimmage on the game field at Gillette Stadium.

It was snowing, the wind was blowing, and it was one of our best practices of the year. Guys really competed. It was the kind of practice you couldn't have during the season, because there's some self-preservation going on, but heading into the Super Bowl, sharpness and preparation wins out over preserving yourself. There's one game left, so what are you saving yourself for? You are preparing to "empty the bucket," as we say. There was great focus, a feeling that we didn't want to have any regrets. I didn't want to look back and say, "I wish I practiced harder. I wish I watched more film." I was willing to do extra that week. We all were.

That week was hard on Tom, but it was also hard on John Jastremski. JJ was our equipment manager, and over the years I'd grown close to him because he was a key part of my daily preparation and especially my game-day prep.

When I was a young player trying to put in extra time to make the transition to wide receiver, JJ was always there for me. In addition to getting everyone's clothing and equipment set, he would come up with drills for me on a daily basis, everything from tennis ball drills to catching playing cards he'd throw at me, JJ was always coming up with something to make me better. When I'd come into the facility at five thirty in the morning, he'd be there before me, ready to go. He'd been with the team since he was in high school, and by now he was in his thirties. I couldn't have become the receiver I did without him.

Because JJ also oversaw preparing the footballs before games, the NFL questioned him repeatedly about the alleged ball deflation. Interview after interview, they really came down hard on him. Yet with everything that was going on, he just kept on doing his job for the team. We continued our drills in Phoenix leading up to the Super Bowl every day. On the road, JJ always had to get imaginative to find us a spot with enough clearance, and one of the spots was a parking lot down the street from the hotel where we'd go early in the morning.

After the NFL's investigation ended a few months after the Super Bowl, the league asked that JJ be suspended. The Patriots complied. In September 2015, after Tom's suspension was overturned, the team was allowed to reinstate JJ. He was reassigned and isn't around the team on a daily basis anymore, but we text and talk still. In 2015, when I had my foot injury, he'd come to my house in Foxborough and I'd sit in a chair while JJ helped me do my tennis balls drills off the retaining wall in my backyard. I truly love the guy for all that. The whole situation during Super Bowl week was tough, and my feeling was that there were enough people asking Tom and JJ questions. I wasn't going to add to it, so JJ and I kept our conversation focused on what I had to do. I wish he were still around. It was tough seeing both a good employee and a good friend no longer be an everyday part of the team. But that week, JJ was worried about keeping everyone else sharp. He worked his ass off for that Super Bowl. That's the way he is.

The week carried on with the predictable pregame hype. I wasn't too interested in all the story lines, because this was truly my first Super Bowl. Against the Giants in Super Bowl XLVI, I wasn't really involved, but this time, I had a role. I had an opportunity to help the team reach its goal of winning its first Super Bowl since the 2004 season.

It wouldn't be easy. Everyone in our locker room knew the Seahawks were the best team we would face all season. We both finished with 12-4 records, but Seattle was the defending Super Bowl champion. The team had a defense that experts considered one of the best of the 2000s. At every level, they were fast and physical: defensive line, linebackers, secondary. They played their cover-3 zone to perfection and had the ability to improvise off of that.

Look at the guys they started on defense in that Super Bowl: Cliff Avril, Michael Bennett, Kevin Williams, Bobby Wagner, Bruce Irvin, K. J. Wright, Richard Sherman, Kam Chancellor, Earl Thomas, Byron Maxwell. That's a lot of Pro Bowls among those guys.

Even though we hadn't played them since 2012—a 24–23 loss that we never should have given away—there was no mystery. Pete Carroll and Dan Quinn, Seattle's defensive coordinator, had their attacking scheme. Guys had latitude to freelance, maybe, but it was all in the framework of the cover-3 scheme. We are a game plan team. We change week to week on both sides of the ball. As I said, it takes a little longer for us to hit our stride sometimes, but when we do, there's a lot to prepare for. We knew how we'd attack Seattle's defense. Those big corners are sometimes a little stiffer. I like those kinds of matchups because I can get squirrelly on them. In 2012, Tom threw it 58 times and Wes had 10 catches for 138 yards. There wasn't going to be much trickery going on. As it is with any good team, it would come down to execution.

For the franchise, being back in Phoenix was coming full circle. This was the same place the Patriots lost Super Bowl XLII against the Giants, 17–14. I couldn't wait for the game to start, so I arrived at the stadium early like I always do, because I have an elaborate pregame routine with ball drills, getting my muscles worked on, taping, taking mental reps, and reviewing the playbook.

When the team was introduced, I took the field as I had all year long: sprinting full out to the opposite end zone. That's something Jerry Rice used to do when he was with the Niners, and I just picked it up from him. It's good to ramp up the RPMs before the game.

I didn't need to run the field to get my motor redlining, though. Just before kickoff, Tom brought us together and poured his heart out to the team with a short speech that spoke to the journey that every one of us had taken to that day. "It's about honor! It's about respect! We win this game, you're honored! Your kids are honored! Your families are honored! Win on three!" It still gives me chills to think about. Everything had been leading to these sixty minutes of football.

Neither team did anything with the ball on its first possession. There was a little feeling-out process. On our second drive, we got moving. I made my first catch over on the left sideline against Byron Maxwell on a comeback route. After the play, there was some talking. From the outside, people might have seen that as disrespect, and sometimes it can be. But not in that game. We had nothing but respect for the Seahawks' team. The chirping was just competitiveness. You're so wired, it has to come out somehow, and that's the way it came out.

I know it comes out a lot with me. I'm expressive and emotional. I like to talk and bump and jump around, and that's going to rub opponents and opposing fans the wrong way. You know what? They need people like me so they can point their finger and say, "That's the bad guy!" as Scarface would say. I play the game 120 percent for my team, and if people don't like that, then they can support who they want to support. I've always been a target for opposing defenses, going back to high school. I'm used to it and I take it as a compliment because it says I'm in their head and I'm good enough to warrant that kind of emotion. You let me bother you, you just gave me power.

Tom chipped away until we faced third-and-6 at Seattle's 10. That's when Michael Bennett made his presence felt. Looping around the right end, he pressured Tom, who had to rush his throw, leading to an easy pick by Jeremy Lane at the goal line. I missed bringing him down at the Seattle 5 but got back after him and caught him at the sideline, diving through his legs to cut him down at the Seattle 13. I lost my helmet on the tackle. I was so pissed there was a pick that I was going full speed while at the same time staying aware of everything around me. When you're chasing down a play like that, you have to stay alert, watching for defensive players who will take your head off while they are blocking. It's the Super Bowl, everyone's going especially hard. Unfortunately, Lane broke his wrist while bracing his fall—the bone actually came through the skin—and he was done for the day. That's something you hate to see happen to anyone.

That play was a big swing. We were on our way to definitely scoring three points, maybe seven. Now those points
were off the board. The defense got us the ball back right
away, though, and we were moving again until we faced
third-and-9 at their 25. Lane's replacement, Tharold Simon,
was covering me. I went in motion left to right and lost him in
traffic. I cooked across the middle of the field and Tom put it
on me in stride. That whole week, we'd placed a huge emphasis on getting upfield right away, because Seattle had such a
fast, swarming defense. "Get vertical" was the key, no hori-
zontal running, so I just put my right foot in the ground and
split the defenders. Two plays later, Tom hit JoJo for the first
points of the game on an under route, which means cutting
in front of, or "under," the linebackers.

Our defense was lights out early in the game, and it wasn't
until late in the half that Seattle tied us on a Marshawn Lynch
touchdown. We'd really moved the ball on them and our
defense had played so well that it felt tough to be tied at that
point. So it was up to us on offense. Our coaches—McDaniels,
O'Shea, Ivan Fears (running backs), and Dave DeGuglielmo
(offensive line)—gave us a great game plan. Seattle was doing
what we thought they would, with the exception of playing
a little more man-to-man coverage. When they slipped into
that, we might have a shot at finding a mismatch. On the next
drive, we did. With thirty-six seconds left, Tom took the snap
at the Seattle 22 and immediately locked in on Gronk, who
was one-on-one with K. J. Wright, a linebacker. Wright's a
good player, but he was out there dealing with two Hall-of-
Fame-level players. Tom dropped it in for the touchdown and
we were back ahead.

We looked good to go into halftime with a lead but suddenly the Seahawks' offense came alive and needed just
twenty-six seconds to go from their 20 to our 11. With just six

seconds left, they tied it again with a touchdown pass from Wilson to Chris Matthews.

At halftime, we knew our plan was working pretty well. We didn't have a lot of points to show for it, because we'd missed a play here and there. That's part of the Super Bowl, when emotions are flying so damn high that you get a little too juiced. Execution was everything, because it can all start with one play. One play creates an opportunity for the next play. A spark gets lit and the playbook opens up.

One other thing about the first half was how intense the competition was. I remember early on going down to block Kam Chancellor, the Seahawks' six-foot-three, 230-pound safety. I popped him and he popped me back and I just thought, *That is a big man.* He was a cool guy to compete against. I'd beat him or he'd beat me and he'd say, "Good play, man." It's fun playing when there's that intensity and that respect. He was like the Gentleman Terminator. And Earl Thomas, Seattle's All-Pro safety, was like a little wolverine out there. A great player, and another guy I loved playing against. That whole defense was so tough and so talented.

I was miked up for the game and I didn't realize until later how much Richard Sherman and I were battling. Sherman is a great corner, and, as he was a fifth-round pick from Stanford who converted to defensive back from receiver, we have a little in common in terms of feeling we have something to prove. In 2012, when we lost to the Seahawks 24–23 in Seattle, Sherman did some gloating at TB. Sherman's one of the loudest, most intense, most intelligent players in the league, and I loved the challenge and I loved letting him know there wasn't anything he could bring at me that I hadn't seen and dealt with before.

I was jacked up, he was jacked up, and we were both doing our thing. There were plenty of plays when I slapped him on his ass and said, "Good play." Other plays, I was MFing him. It's like recess on the playground. You're out there with little Charlie, laughing and having fun, and the next thing you know you're wanting to kill each other. At least that's how I was at recess.

I don't plan anything I say or do, it just comes straight off the top of my dome. I could be talking about a guy's hair or his cleats or his college or where he's from. I'll just say whatever I think will get into someone's head. I usually have a stockpile of material to go at people with, too, because Coach Belichick tests us on our opponents: where they went to school, what their parents' names are, and so forth. I used to have to research punters because I was the returner, and I'd kill him with information: "married his high school sweetheart, college GPA was 3.6 . . ." Finally Coach would say, "OK, that's enough. Obviously you were tipped off on this."

The best trash-talking moment I ever saw was when Bart Scott was on the Jets and he went past our bench and said something to Billy O'Brien. Billy's a fireball and the next thing you know, they're MFing each other; Billy's veins are popping out on his neck—it was amazing, and I was there trying not to laugh.

Looking back at this Super Bowl, I can see that there was definitely a heavy amount of trash talk early because the two teams didn't know each other very well. It was almost like an aggressive introduction going on in the first half.

As the game progressed, guys on both sides were too focused on what they were trying to accomplish to be wasting energy on talking about what they were going to do or what they'd just done.

The third quarter belonged to the Seahawks. They got a field goal off their first drive, then Bobby Wagner, their great linebacker, picked off a throw Tom tried to thread to Gronk.

They put that turnover in the end zone six plays later and we were down 24–14. That's the way momentum can swing in the NFL. Now we needed plays on both sides of the ball to get back into it. That's when Malcolm Butler made his first big play, late in the third, with a big pass breakup on the sidelines to end a drive. We had been in holes during the year and in 2013 and had found a way out. The key was 100 percent focus from everyone, great execution, and situational football. And believing. We believed in Malcolm because we'd seen it since minicamp. And we believed in a guy like Ninko, who made a big third-down sack to stop another Seattle drive early in the fourth. We had a sense of confidence that, "Hey, we can do this."

After that sack, I fielded a punt and got rolled on pretty hard on the tackle, and my right hip went numb. It was a strange sensation and it was difficult for me to get up. That showed up three plays later when we had third-and-14 from our own 28 with 10:58 left.

I was lined up wide to the left, with Dola in the slot next to me. Simon was on me. I ran a deep in-cut and Seattle dropped a bunch of guys into coverage. I saw Tommy step up, and when your quarterback steps up and hasn't thrown it yet, you have a clock in your mind that lets you know you might be taking a hit when the ball arrives. That's what happened. Right as I pulled it in, Chancellor hammered me. My torso bent back over my right side, torqueing that hip as I absorbed the blow. I was braced for it, and because I thought I kept my balance, I popped up and kept running. I was stumbling afterward because of the hip, not because of any hit to the head, which people immediately assumed. And I didn't get up right away, because I was gassed, my hip hurt, and I'd just taken a big hit. More than anything, I was tired.

It was definitely a hard hit—Chancellor lit me up—but if I was knocked out, I wouldn't have been able to keep going.

When I got to the sideline after that drive, the training staff was waiting for me. Honestly, I said to our trainer, Jim Whalen, "Jim, get the fuck away from me! I'm fucking fine! It's Super Bowl Sunday, it's the fourth quarter, we're down seven points, get the fuck away from me! I'll let you know when I'm hurt!"

That didn't matter to them because they have the protocols, and I went through them. I talked to Jim and the independent neurologist, this guy and that guy. They went over and had their little powwow at the video monitor and I was cleared.

From the reaction afterward, you could tell that people didn't realize the other factors. You're in a two-minute drill, you're a receiver, your hip hurts, you've played about sixty plays, you're hyped up—the amount of energy put out in that game is ridiculous. If you watch the film, I'm in the huddle and listening right away for the next play call. I talked fine after the game. People wondered why I didn't get into all the questions I was being asked about the hit and whether I went through protocols. We don't talk about injuries. Point-blank. That's the way we're told to treat it, and I think that's the way it should be. Everyone's medical condition doesn't need to be out there being discussed in public all the time just because we play football.

Meanwhile, four plays later, we faced another third down. On third-and-8 from the Seattle 25, I improvised a little and sat in the middle of the zone coverage. Tom saw me and hit me, then I went vertical fast. My hip still bothered me when I tried to stand, but I was able to run with it. I got down to the 4.

On the next play, I had Simon on me, and I ran a return route in which I'd drive inside, looking like I was going across his face, then stick my foot into the ground and work back outside, returning to the direction I came. It was just like running part of the short shuttle from my pro day at

Kent! We put that play in on the Friday before the game just in case Seattle ran man coverage in the red area. The strength of their corners was they were long, strong, and athletic, but sometimes those guys struggled with quickness and side-to-side direction. If they got their hands on you, that's how they'd win. But Simon's attempt to grab missed and I was open. Tom just missed me. It felt like a missed opportunity, because I didn't know if we'd have a chance to run that again. On the next play, Tom hit Dola for the touchdown and we were within three, 24–21, with eight minutes left.

After a three-and-out for the Seahawks, we got it back at our 36 with 6:52 left. In that situation, we weren't concerned about killing time and leaving them with no time. Bottom line, we had to score. Dola kept saying, "You gotta believe." That was something we'd started saying earlier in the year at random times. We could be in the first quarter of a game and Danny would look at me and say, "You gotta believe," and I'd say, "Danny, you gotta fucking believe," and we'd both break up.

This time, he said it to me, and I said, "I love you, buddy." That was the emotion of the moment. This was what we'd worked for, this moment right there that we were experiencing. It's why we'd run the fucking hill in training camp, it's why we go to LA or Montana to train, it's why in March or April during our time off we put our bodies through maximum effort. All the fucking sweat, all the injuries, all everything, everything came down to that moment. To look in the huddle at the faces, I wanted to say, "Look, I love you guys. Let's fucking go and let's do this." Everyone in there battled something. I was trying to say, "If you are nervous, embrace it. We don't know if we will ever get this opportunity again."

I had the same thought after Super Bowl XLVI, when I saw the older guys in the locker room who hadn't won a championship and didn't that day. Free agents who had been on losing teams their whole career, for who this was potentially their one and only time. You just never know. This was it. And we knew the challenge on the other side. This was the Seattle Seahawks, a badass team. Both teams were laying it on the line right then.

McDaniels called a brilliant last drive. Vereen, who'd been my roommate along with Slates in Foxborough, kept making play after play, and Seattle had no answer for Gronk. When we got inside their 10 and took a time-out, I looked at the clock and there was 2:52 left. I knew this was probably it for our possessions. A Blount run took it to the Seahawks 3, then McDaniels called for the same return route that Tommy and I hadn't connected on the drive before. In the huddle, it was pretty quiet. Everyone was in that zone where this was the whole world. We knew we were on the edge of it. We'd been clawing and scratching to get back and give ourselves a chance, and now we saw the light and we were going to run to it.

I wanted the ball, the chance to put us ahead. I wanted to know that they believed in me. I was praying we'd go back to that play. We did.

Again I had Simon across from me on the line. We both knew I routed him up pretty good the first time on the fake slant portion of the return route. We were in the exact same formation. Would he realize we were running the same play? *You have to be patient*, I thought. *Don't be too quick with it. Let him believe it's a slant under.* I saw the coverage and knew we'd have a shot. As I broke in, Simon tried to hug me up a little and was grabbing, so I leaned on him and popped it back out and I knew I had him. I was wide open. The ball was floating to me. I caught that ball and felt a whirl of emotions. Euphoria. Dola and I smashed heads, and I spiked that thing as hard as I could.

Tom Brady

I had Jules wide open the first time we ran that play at the goal, and it was just a bad throw on my part. I knew where I wanted to throw it, but it's an interesting play. He ran a great route and I sailed it. The next one, I was super confident in him but he was so open I just thought, *Put it on him. Just put it on him!* He sold that inside route perfectly and Simon jumped it pretty good. Jules was very Randy Moss–esque on the forearm shiver and got that separation. Just a great play.

Jules has such a physical style for a guy who's barely two hundred pounds. To take the hit he did from Chancellor, to make the catch and attempt to run for more yards after a hit from one of the hardest hitters in the NFL, shows the kind of physicality he brings. His physical and mental toughness are so high, which is why he's a fit on this team.

I look back at Super Bowl XLIX and realize that Julian was incredible in that game. Huge plays over and over from start to finish at points when we had to have them. It was all pretty storybook stuff, and I still like to remind him, "Do you know you caught the game-winning touchdown in the Super Bowl?" For a kid who grew up in the Bay Area watching Jerry Rice and John Taylor, that's pretty awesome to be able to say.

Up 28–24, we were two minutes from winning the Super Bowl. But right away, Russell Wilson made a play, a thirty-one-yard completion to Marshawn Lynch, and the Seahawks were already on our side of the field at the two-minute warning. The next play was one of the biggest of the Super Bowl: Wilson tried to hit Jermaine Kearse down the seam for a big gain. Malcolm made an incredible play to break it up. After the incompletion, the Seahawks were at the line with eighteen seconds left on the play clock, but they seemed confused. Wilson called time-out just before the play clock hit zeroes. Even though Seattle still had two time-outs left, that burned time-out would play a big role.

After the time-out, Wilson went for it all to Chris Matthews but big Brandon Browner broke that up. I was confident in our defense. I kept thinking, *We'll stop them, we'll stop them.* Then they got that crazy catch from Kearse when it bounced off Malcolm's hand and every one of Kearse's limbs. I was thinking, *How can this happen? Malcolm made a crazy-great play!* Ridiculous.

At our 5 with a minute left, I did the math and considered how much time we'd have left if we let them score so we could get the ball back. That was what we did against the Giants in Super Bowl XLVI. I was just like everyone else: biting my nails, praying for a fumbled snap, a turnover, something!

Seattle called a time-out, then Dont'a Hightower made an unbelievable play to trip up Marshawn before he got to the end zone, bringing him down at the 1. Seattle called another time-out, and this is where that burned time-out after the two-minute warning came into play.

With twenty-six seconds left, if the Seahawks ran it and didn't get in, they'd have to use their last time-out to set up a third-down play. At that point, the option to run the ball would be gone, because they wouldn't be able to stop the clock if it came to fourth down. They'd be in scramble mode with fourth down from the 1 to win the Super Bowl.

At the time I didn't know it, but Coach Belichick saw

Seattle's sideline having a debate about what to do, so he didn't call a time-out, which would have allowed them to get settled. Ballsy. Offensive players don't usually watch when the defense is on the field. We're usually preparing for our next drive. This time, though, everyone was watching. The season hung in the balance.

Seattle ran a play that our scout team had run in practice time after time against our first defense—and had scored almost every time. The design was for the inside receiver, Chris Matthews, to come off the line, drive into Brandon Browner, and create traffic to slow up Malcolm and free up Ricardo Lockette, who would cross behind Matthews. But Browner jammed the hell out of Matthews and there was no traffic. Malcolm didn't hesitate. He'd been locked in for the entire second half and he ended the Super Bowl by driving through Lockette and making the pick.

Talk about an emotional roller coaster. For Malcolm to do what he did on that stage was huge. It felt like a reward for how hard he'd worked.

We exhaled. That was an unbelievable feeling. I saw Dad. I signed "I love you" to him. He signed "I love you" back to me. I started to cry. I thought about how Pops didn't have a dad growing up, about the ground balls that he'd hit to me, the fights we used to get in over sports. I thought about the Redwood City 49ers, Woodside, playing quarterback in college and the transition I'd had to make to have a shot at the NFL, the drive I'd taken to Euclid, Ohio, for pro day training, all of it. As those emotions came to my mind I concentrated on them so I could appreciate the moment.

I don't know if I ever truly thought that I'd get to where I was that day in Phoenix, but I did understand that it was the ultimate emotion an athlete can have, being at the pinnacle of his sport and hoisting that trophy up.

The postgame celebration on the field and into the night was as chaotic as you would think. Confetti flying, friends and family swarming the field, media grabbing the players for interviews, everybody trying to get his hands and lips on the Lombardi Trophy. I talked about Dad in the press conference afterward, and I took a shot at Trent Dilfer for saying we were weak and we weren't good anymore.

One thing that doesn't happen after the Super Bowl? A big postgame locker room celebration. We hustled away to do media for so long that by the time we got back to shower and change, a lot of guys had cleaned up and gone to the after-party. I found myself kicking it with the trainers and the doctors, Slates and Ninkovich. There was a feeling of relief, exhaustion, and exhilaration. Sitting on the chair in front of my locker, peeling off my pads and the tape on my fingers, I felt a wave of fatigue and satisfaction drench me. I was spent. Happy but spent.

I rallied for the party. Rick Ross rapped; I had a few adult beverages with some of my buddies and my family; Gronk danced. I felt like you could go all night and my body just kept saying, "Are you sure?" I spent some quiet time with Tom, visiting him up in his room. Super Bowl XLIX was his sixth time in the final game, so the novelty of a victory party wasn't as big for him. Besides that, after all he'd put in all season, that week and in the fourth quarter, he wanted to spend with his family, which everyone understood.

People don't really realize how tiring a game like that is. Your body has been maxed out. Sometimes in the regular season you feel you're close to redlining in games and you realize how close to total exhaustion you are getting. In the Super Bowl, you get banged up, you see that red line, and you just put the pedal to the metal and blow that bitch if you have to.

The next day, Malcolm and I went to Disneyland. To be

one of the guys who get to go to Disneyland after the Super Bowl? Nothing could beat that. It was a great experience, but they work you there with media and parades all day. And you leave first thing in the morning, so there was a chance I was still a little buzzed when I arrived.

After Disneyland, I headed back to Boston for the parade, flying in late Monday, and people in the airport recognized me and were cheering and dapping me up. I'd always told Brady that if we ever won a Super Bowl we would burn the city down, and we proceeded to do that.

A big snowstorm meant the parade was postponed until Wednesday, so I stayed in Boston and chilled for the day. By the time the parade came I had been in the same clothes for about three days straight. A cop gave Dola and me a ride with sirens blaring through the streets of Boston on the way to the parade; we were halfway out the windows, my beard flapping and people going crazy.

The parade was about what you'd expect. Boston lost its mind for the first Super Bowl since the 2004 season. The number of people to come out after that snowstorm was amazing. I was in a T-shirt, freezing, but I felt like Ferris Bueller up there on the duckboat. Gronk had his Minions hat on, LeGarrette was out there taking selfies, people were firing beers up to us, I got to fire back a little bit at Richard Sherman, who wasn't shy about firing at us when he had a chance. Someone passed me a poster of Sherman from during the game holding up four fingers for the camera. Printed across the poster: "How Many Rings Does Tom Brady Have?" I held that thing up, then knocked it out. I was up there on the duckboat with Dola and Slates and Kurt De La Rosa from Redwood City. We were rolling through the streets of Boston, Super Bowl champions.

What more could I possibly want?

SEVENTEEN

LIFE TAKES A TURN

After the Super Bowl, my life changed a little bit off the field. Disneyland, talk shows, presenting at the Grammys, a cameo in the *Entourage* movie: there were a lot of off-field opportunities coming my way. I was suddenly getting endorsement opportunities from fashion companies, shoe companies, you name it. It was a different world, and I enjoyed it then and still do. I like connecting with fans and doing things that let people see who I am away from football. But you have to do things the right way, always, and there's a lot coming at you.

My Grammy experience was funny in that nobody really knew who the hell I was. I'm just a five-ten white dude walking around in a tux—could be an actor, could be a drummer. I decided to lay low and just observe. It was the musicians' night. Doing *Entourage* was a totally different vibe. There's a lot of downtime doing a movie scene, and I hung with Jeremy Piven, who played Ari Gold, Kevin Dillon (Johnny Drama), and Jerry Ferrara (Turtle) for most of it, shooting the shit. What struck me talking to them was how similar their stories are to the ones I hear in the NFL in terms of having to scratch and fight to get to a level of success. No matter what field you're in, work ethic matters most.

It was fun for a while, but it was important to get back to the routine. Football is the reason people were interested in me in the first place. There was no confusing that. That's my priority. And the 2015 off-season was a tough one for everybody because of what was still going on between Tom and the NFL. In May, the league handed down a four-game suspension for the alleged ball deflation. I thought it was embarrassing, the whole way it went down, but who am I? I'm just a toenail clipping compared with the big dogs in the league office and around the league making the decisions.

On a personal level, though, I felt for Tom. He's a huge part of everything I've achieved. It hurt me because I saw how hurt he was. People don't realize how he is. He loves his family and football. That's it. The guy really doesn't care about anything else. He will go home, play with his kids, put his kids to bed, and then be in bed himself by nine p.m. The dude is so disciplined and does everything right for this league. He stays out of trouble, he's a model citizen, and just because he wins and has success, everyone hates him. Having villains is a part of competitive sports, and I understand how my team is perceived, but it was just unfortunate to see him treated this way.

I understood how angry people in New England were at the league and the commissioner. I was angry. But I also understand there's a lot of politics involved and he had a lot of people to answer to. We all hoped for the best, but at some point, we had to say, "Well, if that's the way it is, then whatever. We'll take care of our business."

Despite all the nonsense, Tom invited a few of us out to Montana to throw with him. It was beautiful. That is God's country up there, being out in a remote spot, where it doesn't get dark until late, with the streams, the trees, the animals, the epic panoramic views—it was a great place to isolate ourselves and train. It wasn't just sitting back having brews on the porch with Tom. It was training, and some golf, too.

We prepared throughout the off-season for Jimmy to be our quarterback for the first four games. I wasn't going to get caught up in the drama of the hearings and appeals and all that. I was there for Tom if he needed me, but the bottom line was we had to prepare for the season. It wasn't until just before the season that Tom's suspension was overturned by Judge Richard Berman.

Obviously, we were all happy. Now it was a matter of getting down to business, and the season started promisingly enough. We scored more than 30 points in seven straight games, and after we beat Washington 27–10 on November 8, we were 8-0. We were so confident. For the first time, I wasn't hurt in any way. The game was really fun. It reminded me of Pop Warner. I was playing well, the team was playing well, we were winning, I was having a good year statistically. But things were turning and we were losing guys to injuries as we went. We lost Nate Solder, our left tackle, against Dallas. We lost Dion Lewis against Washington.

Then we went to play the Giants in New York. We were looking forward to that matchup because the Giants always play us tough, and I liked competing there. I felt fast and explosive and had four quick catches in the first quarter and then—*bam*—I got hurt. It was terrible. I broke my foot again.

I remember the play. I was one on one with a safety and I felt I had a chance to blow by him. But after the catch, he had a kung fu grip on my jersey, and the Giants' linebacker Jasper Brinkley arrived. I tried to slow down and swing the safety off me, but Brinkley was on me, too, and all the weight on my foot was too much. I didn't feel a pop. It was sore but I could walk on it, so I thought it was a midfoot sprain. After all the tests on the sideline, though, the medical staff wanted to take a closer look and make sure. When the X-ray came back, the injury was obvious.

My foot was going to keep me down for a while, but I was determined to come back for the playoffs once I had a timetable for healing. But it was so tough to watch us after that. We got to 10-0 before we lost our first game, on the road, in the snow in overtime against the Broncos.

All of a sudden, we were in trouble. The injuries on both sides of the ball were piling up. We knew how good we were when we had everyone out there, but you can't use injuries as an excuse. Every team gets them. You just have to play through them. We lost four of our last six games, which is really uncommon for our team, because we usually peak late in the year.

Our first playoff game was against the Chiefs in Foxborough. I had ten catches for 100 yards in a 27–20 win, but it wasn't me out there, by any stretch. I was playing with huge cleats to protect my foot and I couldn't cut with confidence. But our team had been banged up before, and I held out hope that we'd be able to pull through.

Unfortunately, Denver was no joke that year, especially on defense. We went to Mile High Stadium for the AFC Championship, but that game reminded me of the conference championship after the 2013 season. We just didn't have it that day, and the Broncos were playing so well with Peyton at quarterback. He wasn't throwing the ball all over the place, he was managing situations and taking advantage when he saw something. It was a tribute to how smart he was as a quarterback, because he wasn't physically able to do as much as he previously could. We almost pulled out a win thanks to an amazing fourth-quarter effort. Great situational football put us in position to tie it at the end after we'd been turned away twice deep in Denver territory. But we lost 20–18 when Tom's pass to me on a two-point conversion attempt was picked off.

They outplayed us. I hate going to Denver and I hate losing. Other than that, I don't even like to think about that game, because if we'd won it, we'd have played in Super Bowl L in Santa Clara. Instead, it was the Broncos and the Panthers.

The only other thing worth mentioning from that disappointing season was what happened at the Super Bowl, and not on the field. The NFL invited all the MVPs from previous Super Bowls to be introduced on the field in a celebration of the game's golden anniversary. When Tom was introduced, boos came down from everywhere.

Later that night, I got a text from him. It read, "Everyone fucking hates us. Let's win it all next year."

Of course, I was with Tom all the way, but we had a long road in front of us. First, the 2016 off-season was probably the most stressful of my life, on both the personal and professional fronts. I learned that my foot hadn't properly healed and that I needed my fourth foot surgery since 2012. It was a huge blow and bad déjà vu for me. In 2012, after breaking my right foot against Miami, the bone didn't heal properly around the inserted screw, requiring a second surgery. It was happening again. The odds were that just one in five patients needed a second surgery if the screw didn't take. I was again the one in five. If the second surgery didn't solve the problem, my recovery would be very complicated.

Meanwhile, in May I would turn thirty, a milestone birthday in the NFL since the overwhelming majority of players in the league are younger than that age. It's a young man's game, and teams are always looking to upgrade or save money against the league's salary cap. Even if there wasn't pressure being applied by the Patriots, I knew the landscape well enough to understand that, when and if I recovered, I'd better be able to make plays. The fear that, "Hey, they are going to move on from me," never really fades. You just never know. I've seen a lot of crazy shit over my nine-year career in New England, and nobody is exempt.

The day before my second surgery, my personal life changed dramatically. I found out I was going to be a father. A woman I spent a brief time with was due in December. The realization that I would be responsible for a child was obviously on a different level from my foot and football, and it was a complicated situation, too. It's one thing if you are in a relationship with someone and she becomes pregnant. It's another thing when you aren't familiar with someone and learn you are going to have a child with her. No one ever dreams of that. I come from a tight family and the way I'd envisioned fatherhood was far different. There were so many different emotions: concern for the baby, knowing I would need to be there to love and provide for her, and also feeling that I'd let my family down. I couldn't tell my parents for a while, because I was terrified of their reaction.

My life to that point had been about me. To prepare and perform in the NFL, I felt I needed to be mentally engaged 100 percent with the game. I had great respect for the family guys on the team like Tom, Vince Wilfork, Jerod Mayo, Logan Mankins, and Nate Solder. So many of them are able to be great dads and great players. Could I? I didn't know how to handle it. I felt like I'd been hit by a tidal wave.

I began seeing a therapist. In the past, I'd consulted sports psychologists who helped me with my focus and performance. But these sessions with the therapist were about settling my mind. I needed a nonbiased opinion on all the different things I was feeling, and advice on how to process them. As I dealt with my feelings of helplessness and loss of control, like my life was upside down personally and professionally, I would have days with horrible mood swings. I tried to battle it by making a routine and sticking by it. That helped.

In the morning, I'd go to TB12 Sports Therapy in Foxborough, right near the stadium. Alex Guerrero would work on me, then I'd go back to TB12 at night. In between, I'd work out, do some time in a sleep tank to help with my recovery, handle all my off-field responsibilities, nap, see my psychiatrist on Thursdays, and then do it again.

Tom was such a good help for me mentally, really like a brother. He was a shoulder I could lean on. I had a lot of good friends helping me throughout, and when I finally told my parents, I was surprised how supportive they were.

That was hard because I'd held it from them, and the pressure of the situation was making it harder to open up. One day, Dad said to me on the phone, "A lot of people in the world have real-life problems that are harder to deal with than having a bad practice or a foot that hurts." At that point, I told him what was weighing on me. I think it hurt Mom and Dad that I felt I couldn't turn to them for support and advice. Dad said, "I'm your best friend, you can tell me anything. We all have things happen in life that are complicated and not what we planned, but that's life."

My relationship with my father went to a different level. He said, "You just worry about football right now. This is all going to be all right. We are going to help you with every single step of this, and that baby isn't going to lack any love. We are going to do the right thing, the responsible thing." Hearing that took a huge weight off my shoulders.

Once you have a kid yourself, you realize that your mom and dad always wanted the best for you. Thinking about all those things they used to bitch you out for or ground you over, you slowly begin to realize that, "Man, they were just trying to mold me and make me a better person."

Meanwhile, Tom had his own issues to deal with. In early March, the US Second Circuit Court of Appeals heard the NFL's Deflategate appeal. At the end of April, the three-judge panel ruled in favor of the league. The ruling didn't confirm any of the NFL's findings. But it did rule that NFL commissioner Roger Goodell had the power to suspend Tom based on the collective bargaining agreement between the owners and players. The four-game suspension was back in place.

In July, Tom dropped his appeal entirely and accepted the four-game suspension. It had gone on for so long and the chances of its being overturned a second time were so small, Tom felt like it just needed to end. As I've said, it was extremely difficult to watch this as a friend. He was our best player and one of my best friends. I hurt for him.

There were days Tom was quiet in the locker room, but he's a closed book when he wants to be and in this case, he wasn't talking about the situation. I would joke around with him, bust his balls or make a joke about missing him, but I respected that he needed space, too. More than anything, I said, "I'm here if you need me."

Tom is the most mentally tough guy I have ever seen, and that's who I strive to be like. That's part of the reason speaking with a doctor helped me so much. I needed to learn how to compartmentalize my thoughts. For Tom, when it's football time, it's football time. The suspension obviously affected football and that's what hurt.

Part of my role with the change at quarterback was setting an example. Having been with the team as long as just about anyone, my reaction would send a message that I knew could rub off on younger guys. My job was to support the backup quarterback, Jimmy Garoppolo, and make sure that everyone knew, at that moment, that Jimmy was the guy. I'm loyal to Tom. But Tom would do the same thing that I had to do. I felt bad for Tom and hated the entire situation, but I am still paid to go out and win ball games and do my job.

The thing I appreciated about Jimmy was the confidence about him. He could screw something up in practice and then go out and try the same thing and execute it in a game. He's got that swagger, and he also isn't afraid to work. I've trained with him in the off-season, and he keeps up. I was proud of the way he handled himself in a very hard situation. He commanded attention in the huddle and was demanding of us on the field.

I was going to do everything to help him out and make sure that he knew he had my support. It wasn't my job to coach him. I wasn't going to tell him, "Do this, do that," because I don't know what he was being told by his coach. It was my job, though, to go in there and work with him and talk with him just as if he were Tom. That was my loyalty to the team.

There were a lot of new faces in the locker room in 2016, and many of them were hungry to taste success. Chris Long, a defensive end, had been in the league since 2008 but had never been to the playoffs. Martellus Bennett, a big tight end with an eccentric personality, hadn't fit in other spots and had played in only one playoff game. Another big one was Chris Hogan, a wide receiver we signed as a restricted free agent from the Bills.

They worked their asses off. I knew Chris Long a little through Dola, who'd played with him at the Rams. I went to some concerts with him and hung out and found that Chris is a very charismatic guy, really intelligent but always pretty chill. Perfect locker room guy. Marty B. was beautifully unique. You never knew what he'd say. I learned so much from him in terms of creativity, business, and life outlook. At the same time, he worked his ass off on the field. He played hurt, was a big factor in the passing game, and blocked hard; he was a guy you just felt happy to be around.

One of my favorite things about Marty was when Coach Belichick would ask a rhetorical question in a team meeting, Marty would answer it. And it would be a good answer, so everyone would look at Marty, then at Coach, to see how he was going to react. Then Marty would look around and say, "What?! Am I wrong?!" He'd also come out with the most random suggestions when we were putting in verbal signals. I can't give an example because I'm not giving anything away, but they were usually hysterical. Remember in school when there was the class clown who distracted, and the class clown who actually advanced things? That was Marty. The smart class clown.

Chris was funny in his own way, too, because he's such a no-bullshit kind of guy who will say how he feels regardless. I've been a Patriot my whole career and there are things I would never say or do because it might not go over well with Coach Belichick. It's funny to watch a guy like Chris come in and ask point-blank, "Why do we do this?" or, "Wouldn't this be better?" It's interesting when players join our team after a career somewhere else, because you hear their perspectives on things and what they think of the way we do things.

For the wide receivers, adding Hogan and a rookie receiver from Georgia, Malcolm Mitchell, had a huge effect on our group. Those two pushed all of us and brought out an even higher level of competition in the receiver group. All they wanted to do was learn, train, and play. Our receiver room was one of the best I've been a part of. The whole locker room was that way. Guys weren't creating distractions with their own bullshit.

Everyone has personal goals and everyone wants things to go their way. But once a guy starts to put that out there, to show it, that's when it becomes a negative and a distraction. The fact that Tom is so completely team-first in everything sets the tone. Everyone knows his story and how he had to wait for his chance and how hard he worked. When you see him, after all he's accomplished, working the way he does and sacrificing, you know the standard.

Tom's suspension went into effect on September 3. Once he left the facility that Saturday, that was it. We wouldn't see him again until October 3. No calls, no texts, no contact. The last thing I said to him when he left: "We got you, bro. The machine will be gassed up and oiled, waiting for you when you get back."

We opened the season at Arizona on *Sunday Night Football*. There wasn't a "Let's win it for Tom!" mind-set, but there was a sense of urgency. We all knew we had to do our job at a very high level because we were missing our best player.

At the beginning of the year, I was a lot better than I was during the 2015 playoffs, but I still didn't feel sharp. The process of coming back from an injury meant I was still getting used to how I felt in a game environment. You can go to practice and ball out and do all that stuff, but in a game, getting tackled or struggling for extra yards, there's about a 20 percent increase of exertion.

We learned a lot about our team that night in Arizona. Jimmy played great. He ran the offense, he was in command, and he was accurate as hell. We all felt good for him. But the biggest thing was the resilience, coming from behind to win 23–21. After the game, NBC's sideline reporter Michele Tafoya asked me on the air if I had anything to say to Tom. We weren't supposed to have any contact with him, but I figured I'd be able to get away with a broadcast message, so I said into the camera, "Love you buddy! We're gonna get a couple more for ya!"

Which is what we did.

The home opener was against Miami, and we were all over them, getting up 24–0 before halftime. But Jimmy got hurt in the second quarter when the Dolphins' linebacker Kiko Alonso drove him into the turf on a third-down completion to Malcolm Mitchell, separating his shoulder. The next man up was the rookie Jacoby Brissett. It got tight down the stretch and the final was 31-24, but we were 2-0 without Tom and had now beaten a division opponent without him, Gronk, Dont'a Hightower, and—for most of the game—Jimmy. The win showed a lot of mental toughness.

With Jimmy unable to go against Houston, suddenly I was the backup at quarterback behind Jacoby as we prepared for the Texans. Honestly, I was excited. In the moment I saw Jimmy get hurt, I thought, *That sucks for Jimmy, he was playing well. That means Jacoby is in, and now we'll see what he's about. Shit, I think I'm the backup quarterback. That's dope. What if I have to play? What if I make a great play? What if I make a great play and we win?*

I didn't want anything to happen to Jacoby, but it gave me a good kind of anxiety to know that I had that on my plate that week.

I was in the protection meetings so I would understand the line calls and the blitz pickups and blocking schemes, and there was a package of plays set aside for me. Worst case, I'd be able to run around. Let's be realistic, I couldn't throw the football like an NFL QB. They are too damn good and I was out of practice. But I could probably have run around if I had to.

There was a lot going through my head that week, but it was for nothing. Jacoby, being the stud that he was, was able to get us through that game against Houston. With him and our lights-out defense, we won 27–0. It would have been sweet to win all four games without Tom, but we ran out of gas in the last one against the Bills, losing 16–0.

The next day, even after the loss, we kind of had that first-day-of-school feeling. We'd be able to see our boy for the first time in a while.

Tom strolled in with a little smile on his face, but you could see he was super serious, too, by the way he was moving. All week long, I kept starting a little Brady chant when he came into the locker room. I'd start out soft, "Bra-dy . . . Bra-dy . . . Bra-dy. *Bra-dy!*" Then get up to screaming, "BRA-DY! BRA-DY! BRA-DY!" and jump on him. He'd be saying, "Enough, bro. Enough!"

All week, the energy was through the roof. After a great week of practice, we headed to Cleveland to play the Browns.

Tom played unbelievably. That day was just a case of Tom Brady being Tom Brady and, honestly, I expected nothing less. He went out and threw for 406 yards and hit Martellus with three touchdown passes as we won 33–13.

With the band back together, we started rolling. We beat the Bengals at Gillette, then won on the road against Pittsburgh and Buffalo to go into the bye at 7-1.

Everything was headed in the right direction. Then came one of those "Holy shit!" personnel moves. Jamie Collins was traded to Cleveland on Halloween. I'd been on the team for a while. I was there when Richard Seymour was traded, when Randy Moss was traded, when Logan Mankins was traded. It's always a shock initially to lose a teammate, but it's never a surprise when Coach Belichick makes a business decision you didn't see coming.

He's done it time and again, so Jamie wasn't the first, and he won't be the last. Coach Belichick is going to do what he feels is the best for the team, and as a player, you have to support it even if you love the guy. We don't always know the big picture. That doesn't mean we don't say, "Fuck, that's crazy!" but that stays in our locker room and building. We know not to cross that boundary. We all have opinions, but the sheer volume of results showing that Coach Belichick knows what he's doing trumps any opinion. That's how I think about it when Bill makes a move like that. *Damn, he may be nuts, but it's probably going to work out.*

Coming out of the bye we had a rematch with the Seahawks, our first time seeing them since Super Bowl XLIX. Anytime you play against a team like Seattle, it's a measuring-stick game. You want to play the best teams to see where you are. That's only natural. We didn't play well that game and made a lot of mistakes—I had a costly fumble that led to the go-ahead touchdown—but there was a sense that, "Hey, if we just clean up these stupid mistakes, we're a pretty good team." But you can't afford mistakes against a team like Seattle. If you make them, you lose, and we did, 31–24.

As miserable as losing to the Seahawks was, our next game was a big one for me. We went back to the bay to play the 49ers.

I was injured in 2012 when we lost to the Niners at Gillette, so this was my first time playing against the team I grew up watching. Being able to go home and see my family during the season and play in front of friends and family for the first time since I was at the College of San Mateo in 2008 was something I was looking forward to once the schedule came out.

I felt like I knew half the stadium. I bought about thirty-five tickets, and even though it wasn't Candlestick, where I grew up going to games, it was still the Niners. Walking through the facility, I saw pictures of all the greats: Joe Montana, Steve Young, Jerry Rice, Tom Rathman, Brent Jones,

Roger Craig, Ken Norton, Deion Sanders, Charles Haley. These were guys I grew up idolizing.

When I was a kid, Redwood City Pop Warner would have a day where we all went to the game. We'd be in the section of bleachers that was pulled out over the baseball field at the 'Stick. We had the worst seats in the house, but you could go to the end of the bleachers and see the behind-the-scenes stuff as the players prepared to come onto the field. We'd be pressed up against the fence, excitedly looking for Steve Young and Rice. This wasn't the 'Stick, but it was still home.

It was a special day, and the Niners' stadium personnel made it special, saying, "Welcome back, Mr. Edelman . . ." when I walked past. I remember talking to some of the security guards and having them tell me I played against their friend or their cousin back at Woodside. It was just a daylong trip down memory lane for me, and it was a thrill to score the game's first touchdown on a little four-yard dart from Tom.

It was a big game for him, too, being back home. He was injured in 2008 the last time the Patriots played the Niners in SF. Over the years, I've gotten to know Tom's family pretty well, and they are special people. Tom's mom, Galynn, is a very gentle and caring person and Tom Sr. is a San Mateo guy who brings a warmth with him. They all make you feel comfortable. I remember meeting his sisters when I was a rookie, and they were all so respectful and nice to me when I was some nobody on the team.

While I was dealing with a lot that year, Tom also had his own share of personal issues. Galynn had been sick since before training camp, so Tom was dealing with both the suspension from the league and her illness. This again showed his mental toughness and ability to compartmentalize. He's got a poker face that's second to none. I don't really remember him ever having a bad week of practice mentally or emotionally because of it. He was on a mission in 2016. I don't know what the mission was; it could have been for his mother or for revenge or both. We never really talked about it, and I think that's the way he wanted it. When he comes into the facility, he has fun with the fellas, prepares, and works.

Next up, we had the Jets on the road. Even though we'd had a run of success in the AFC East, divisional games are always difficult because we all know each other's personnel so well. You play twice a year, every year. There aren't a lot of surprises in those games; rather, it's about execution. The rivalry factor is also very real. I'm sure that the Dolphins, Bills, and Jets are pretty tired of us winning the division. It's not hard to work up a dislike for each other. So this was another hard-fought divisional game that we battled from behind to win, 22–17.

We also took a big hit in this one. In the first quarter, Gronk left the field after he was landed on while diving for a pass from Tom in the first quarter. Gronk had also taken a big hit the week before from the Seahawks' safety Earl Thomas and had gotten a bruised lung. This time, it was his back. And it turned out to be a season-ender. It was crushing news. We knew how hard he worked to get back from all the injuries he suffered. Now he was in line for another surgery and rehab. People don't understand how hard it is to have a season ended by injury. All the work you put in during the off-season, in training camp, in practice every week, and then you realize you won't be a part of the team in a meaningful way for the rest of the year. It really bothers you personally to see a friend go through that.

Heading into December we were 9-2. We were focused on closing the season better than 2015 and hitting our peak as the season wound down. While people outside our team were talking about us being on a "Revenge Tour" and things like that, believe me, we weren't talking that way. Coach Belichick does a damn good job of not letting that stuff get into our minds. Every meeting, every practice, he reminds us of all the shit we have to do. The urgency he creates for each week's game makes it so we don't have time to think about anything but that week's game.

When you're on the team long enough, you know there are things you just don't discuss, and talking about what the team wants to ultimately accomplish is one of those things. What I do know is that Coach wants me to play consistently well. That's really the only thing I know about him, and that's the truth. He's the ultimate coach/businessman/general. You don't know what cards he is holding. I've counted the cards and I still don't know! Coach is all about winning ball games. It's unreal. His attitude trickles down so that it becomes a model for everyone else to follow. That's how it sticks. We follow his lead, and the guys who come onto the team, whether they're rookies or veterans, get it pretty quickly.

We entered the playoffs on a seven-game winning streak and finished the regular season 14-2. I finished the year with 98 catches for 1,156 yards, the most receiving yards I'd ever had. All nice numbers, but none of that really mattered once we wrapped up the season.

The message was now, "We haven't done anything. We're 0-0. We are not a finished product." It helped maintain that sense of urgency for a team that was still young, with a lot of players who hadn't been in the playoffs before. You are always trying to improve, shape, and form your team. You aren't done with that, really, until you've arrived at the Super Bowl. That's when the team is the team.

I was in a much better place in my personal life by the end of the season than I was in the spring. I flew back to California on November 30 to see the birth of my daughter, Lily Rose Mary Edelman. To experience that was a huge weight off my shoulders. Once you hold your little nugget in your arms, your life has changed.

I didn't know what real love was until I held her. I realized I was going to be a huge part of who she would become, by my actions and decisions and how she was raised. I clearly came from a strong household and experienced an ideal upbringing. To have a child out of wedlock wasn't something I grew up seeing myself doing, but having Lily as a part of my life and my parents' lives has been a blessing. Lily isn't lacking for love, that's for sure.

I was in a much better place physically, too. Entering the postseason, my body actually felt stronger. It takes a long time to figure out what your body needs, and what I've discovered in the last few years is that I need rest. During the season, I'll do flotation therapy twice a week. As the season progresses, I may go three or four times a week. When I first heard about flotation therapy—also called sensory deprivation therapy—in 2014, I was skeptical, but the sessions make an incredible difference in my weekly recovery. The flotation tanks are like big coffins filled with heated saltwater so that you float easily. It's like lying on a cloud, and you feel 100 percent relaxed. My nutrition has improved since I've been in the league, too, and I credit Alex Guerrero for a lot of that. He's been a huge help in my career, just working on my body to make it more pliable and making sure my diet is balanced and I'm getting the right supplements and vitamins for my joints, circulation, and recovery. My feet are my tools, and I've already had two surgeries on both of them. Alex keeps them in working order, rubbing them out before practice to get them ready and after practice to flush them out. If you don't keep the muscles pliable and you don't keep your body hydrated, you're not giving yourself the best chance to succeed. It truly makes a difference for me.

In the divisional playoffs, we were up against the Houston Texans and their excellent defense. We'd beaten them 27–0 with Jacoby at quarterback in week 3, but we knew it wouldn't be easy against Billy O'Brien's team in the playoffs. It wasn't. We broke away from a 17–13 halftime lead to win 34–16, but there was plenty from that game we needed to do better if we wanted to stick around in the playoffs.

That win earned us a trip to our sixth-straight AFC Championship Game. Obviously, that's an accomplishment we're proud of, but I don't think there's a sense that we matched the guys that came before us. The Tedy Bruschis, Troy Browns, Kevin Faulks, Mike Vrabels, that generation of guys won three Super Bowls in 2001, 2003, and 2004. We'd won one at that point, so we were still in the shadow of those men and their legacies. Those dudes are legends. Three Super Bowls! I've thought of it before: *What if our generation could be like that?* Getting to six straight AFC Championships doesn't match three Super Bowls. The conference championships you lose? You don't even remember them.

We hosted the Steelers on January 22. The winner would play the Falcons in Houston. Honestly, I love playing Pittsburgh. It's always such a battle, and I love the tradition. Going to Kent State, where there were a ton of Steelers fans and playing for the same program that produced those great Steelers linebackers Jack Lambert and James Harrison, I just have a lot of respect for them and their ownership family, the Rooneys. If you're a fan of the game, the Pittsburgh franchise gets your juices flowing.

We played really well, winning 36–17. Chris Hogan had a huge game, and I was so happy for him. He was a great addition to our offense, finishing with 180 yards receiving and two touchdowns. I had 118 yards on eight catches and scored a late touchdown to make it 33–9.

When it ended and the confetti flew, we were happy, but my mentality was that there was still some meat on the bone. I'd been to the Super Bowl and lost. I'd been to the Super Bowl and won. It was a business mind-set for all of us, I think. We hadn't come that far just to come that far. Standing on the field, I was already thinking of Atlanta, though I had no idea we were walking into one of the most epic Super Bowls in history.

EIGHTEEN

A HELLUVA STORY

When there are just two teams left, the media and fan focus is invariably more intense. For our franchise, with Tom, Coach Belichick, and our history in the Super Bowl, the focus gets multiplied. That's not even taking into account all the stories and speculation about finishing off this so-called Revenge Tour because of Deflategate and what it would mean for Tom to win.

Having played in these types of games before gave us an advantage. We knew how to focus, and that meant actively deciding not to get caught up in it. For me, I was already on the "let's prepare" program before the confetti hit the ground at Gillette. I'd bought in to the mind-set of, "Fuck everything else, just try to improve every day."

The week before we left for Houston, I was doing the exact same thing I always do: film, lift, rest, focus, treatment, and ignore the noise. Did I know what the game meant to Tom? Of course. And as a guy, a friend, and a teammate who I'd worked with for eight years at that point, I knew all Tom had gone through, between his mom's illness and the suspension. We didn't sit around and have meetings about it like people seemed to think we did, but there was definitely thought given to the fact it would be pretty cool if we could get this done for him. Winning might not cure everything, but it's good medicine.

There was one storyline that emerged before we left for Houston that lingered through the week of the Super Bowl. I am a white guy. Dola and Chris Hogan are also white guys. I understand there are more black guys that play receiver than white guys, but I wasn't into looking for the deeper meaning behind it all or what it says about society.

To me, when somebody says something about me being a white receiver, it feels like it discredits me somehow. I've always used all that bullshit as fuel. And that's all it really is: bullshit. I've been dealing with being underestimated athletically because I'm white my whole life. Or people thought I was black when they saw me on film at Woodside or the College of San Mateo because of my playing style and my name. In fact, when I arrived at Kent, all the white kids told me they thought I was a black kid until they met me.

Just because the circumstances and stage are bigger, it doesn't mean I handle it any differently. My feeling has always been, "All right, let's go out and play ball and find out." It doesn't consume me by any stretch, but you always want to prove the haters wrong.

Matt Slater

People have had a hard time accepting that Julian is one of the best wide receivers in the league, but I don't think you can argue that now. You look at his body of work and you can see that he produces as well as anyone. I know he gets categorized because he's white, but I would put him up there with anybody in the league. I don't think that he gets enough credit. We have in our mind a picture of what a receiver looks like. We picture six foot four, 220 pounds, probably going to be a black guy, and I think when people see Julian playing receiver, or any white skilled players, there is a tendency to say, "Well, this guy can't be as skilled as the brothers that are doing it." That isn't fair at all. Jules has obviously broken a lot of those stereotypes. He is an athlete who can compete at a high level against anyone. People need to see past the color of his skin, and once they do I think he will start to be appreciated a little bit more.

Even though we hadn't played Atlanta since that *Sunday Night Football* win early in 2013, we were familiar with the Falcons' defensive scheme because their head coach was Dan Quinn, who with Pete Carroll had built the Seahawks' defense we'd gone up against in Super Bowl XLIX. After that game, Quinn took over Atlanta, so, as you'd expect, there was a strong resemblance between the two defenses.

The Falcons were fast at every level. In the secondary, their guys had great length, which means they were tall and lean, with long arms. Just like the Seahawks, they swarmed the football, so it was a point of emphasis that we got vertical on them when we had the ball. If you run side to side against a team with speed like the Falcons, you're just going to get caught from behind and swarmed under. We were expecting aggressiveness, a fundamentally sound defense, and that drop-zone coverage in which everyone had an area to patrol. We knew it was going to be a fast game and that, if they had the chance, they would rip at the football and try to create turnovers.

We had three practices and a long walk-through before we left for Houston late Monday morning, January 30. It was important to get our bodies in prime shape during that time, so that meant massage, extra treatment, and some extra lifting. During the season, we don't really have a chance to lift hard, because we're in between recovering from one game and preparing for the next. The week off before the Super Bowl allows you to get a couple of lifts in later in the week so you're feeling strong before you fly.

By the time we got on that plane, our game plan was set. We hadn't played well against the Texans in the divisional playoff, and the Steelers hadn't really played their best against us in the AFC Championship, we knew that. There was an urgency to our practices. We didn't think we had everything figured out, not by any means.

Our first practice was at the University of Houston on Wednesday. We went for two hours and, because of the work we'd done back home the week before, we got into situational football, red zone work, and two-minute offense. That practice in particular, I remember loving the energy and the urgency. Going from freezing Massachusetts to warm Houston in late January put a little bounce in our step. We'd been outside all year long for practice in Foxborough, and that's not always fun when the ground is frozen and it's rainy, windy, or snowing. All of a sudden, we were someplace warm, and it was like a field trip. It rejuvenated the body a little bit.

We had lighter practices on Thursday and Friday and, on Saturday, we went to NRG Stadium for a very brief walk-through, team pictures, and a chance to be with our friends and families on the field.

I hung around with my folks and family and had the chance to see my teammates' families, but being a day away from the game, I got a gnawing feeling I wanted to out. I'm such a creature of habit, I wanted to get back to the hotel and begin my routine. Fortunately, my family knows that, so when the walk-through ended, I was in game prep mode and didn't have any interruptions.

When I got back to the hotel, I got my body work done then took a walk around the area nearby. I find walking helps still my mind and remove the clutter that pushes in sometimes, and I do it a lot when we're on the road, whether it's around the hotel or just down into some random neighborhood.

I just relaxed. Got my body work done. Took a walk. I like to be by myself. Walk around the facility or the hotel. Throughout the day, I ate constantly. You burn so much energy all day during a Super Bowl, you need the fuel in the system. I spent time with Dola shooting the shit about the game and the game plan.

On Super Bowl Sunday I was up by six a.m. Bobby Cole, who took over for JJ as equipment assistant and my personal tennis ball-drill coordinator, needed to be at the stadium by seven thirty, so he and I went to the hotel parking garage and ran through my workout. It takes about forty-five minutes to an hour to get it all done, depending on how it goes. I'll catch one-handed off the wall, then catch with a ball in my opposite hand. Then I'll catch color-coordinated balls that, depending on the color, I have to catch with a certain hand. We use reaction balls that take crazy bounces, harder balls that come off fast. I'll catch reaching across my body, over my shoulder, balls thrown directly at my chest or face. It's constant firing, and the hand-eye coordination and concentration help me get my brain going.

Little did I know how much the six a.m. drills I did with Bobby in that parking garage would help me fifteen hours later, when our season was hanging in the air in the fourth quarter!

I went over to the stadium on one of the early buses. There is nothing worse for my anxiety than feeling rushed, so to stay out of that bad place, I'm always one of the first ones to arrive. That gives me time to just chill and even take a thirty-minute power nap if I need it. At Gillette, we have sleep rooms, but on the road I'll have to be resourceful and find a quiet nook or place where I won't get stepped on. I ran through my mental punch list of things to do: eat right away, drink a coffee to get a little caffeine in me—not too much—check out the socks laid out for me and pick two pairs, then find the right tights for the day to wear under my game pants. I took my quick shower and then let Bobby know I was almost ready to go onto the field for our pregame warm-up. After I taped my fingers and got my headphones on, we headed to the field.

The first few moments, I eased into the workout, getting used to the field conditions and oriented to the play clock and the scoreboard. Being there early allowed me to ease into the day and my routine. Even though it was the last game of the year, something that we'd built to and dreamed about and knew a lot of the planet would be watching, I still stick to the routine. It's part of who I've always been, that routine. The drills might be different now, but the preparation time is the same for almost any game I've ever played, and it definitely goes back to the foundation Dad laid for me.

The atmosphere in a Super Bowl stadium is electric hours before the game even starts. Everywhere you look, there are celebrities and former players milling on the sidelines. There's a thickness in the air at those games that I can feel. I appreciate how big it is, but I have to hold back and remind myself, *Hey, you've got a job to do. This is not an event for us, this is work.* The more I remind myself of that, the more normal the game feels.

The locker room before the game was the same as it always is, which is pretty businesslike. There will be a couple of quiet high-fives and some quiet conversation, but it's not real loud. Guys who listen to music have it in their headphones.

We take our cues from Coach Belichick, I think, and he's not one for being demonstrative. Banging your head against the locker isn't going to help anyone play better. Being prepared will.

We felt well prepared. We had two good weeks of practice. We knew what we wanted to do. We felt good about our plan.

We knew we had to play better against Atlanta than we had against Houston and Pittsburgh. Then the Falcons punched us in the face. Big punch. Haymaker. Part of me was thinking, *What the fuck, we had a good week of practice, what are we doing?* but there were also adjustments to make. To their credit, the Falcons didn't come out and do exactly what they always do. They had a whole different plan, and they were executing it well. They went after Tom hard and they worked to keep bodies buzzing around me. After a stretch in the middle of the regular season in which the ball was getting spread around a lot, my targets had gone up steadily. Tom threw to me 111 times in the nine games before the Super Bowl.

Their scheme was smart. Pressure Tom and take away the guy working underneath. That was me. This guy dropped with me, that guy bumped me, another guy was shading me. We had to adjust. We just had to plain out-execute them, and we weren't doing that. We moved the ball on them. In the first quarter, we got down to their 40 before we had to punt, and on our third possession, I had a twenty-seven-yard catch to get us down to their 30 when the game was still scoreless.

But right after that, their rookie linebacker Deion Jones ripped the ball off LeGarrette Blount to end the drive. That's when Matt Ryan and Julio Jones heated up. Julio is no question one of the best in the NFL—he's just so athletic and has such amazing body control and toughness—and Matty started getting him for chunks. It wasn't that we weren't in position defensively, either. The Falcons were just executing. Our offense wasn't. The Falcons went up 7–0. After a three-and-out for us, they made it 14–0.

I sat on the bench thinking, *We talked about all this. We talked about how they liked to strip the ball. We talked about being ready to make adjustments. We talked playing from ahead because the Falcons don't like playing from behind.* We were doing the exact opposite of our focal points from the week of practice. So I sat there and said to myself, *OK, let's get back and do the shit that we are supposed to do. Let's not try to go above and beyond.* McDaniels was preaching that as the first half went along: "Let's not try to make this insane play. Let's just make the plays we are supposed to make. Let's just play how we play."

We took the field down 14–0, and there was no panic. We took over at our 25, and the aggressiveness Atlanta showed on our first three drives was still there. They got whistled for three defensive holds to help us make it down to their 23. Then, on a third-and-6, Dola and I ran a combo underneath a route designed to get us the first down. I came in motion from the outside left to the left slots. and at the snap, ran a shallow cross. Dola crossed around behind me to the left, then cut back to trail me. Atlanta played a coverage called lock-and-combo. Tom could see the secondary converging on me a corner coming on my left up, and a "robber"—meaning an extra defender—lurking right in my path. If Tom came to me, there was going to be a Falcons' team meeting. He went to Dola, and he would have picked up the first down. The problem was, Robert Alford made a great play. He jumped the route and showed up where Tom didn't expect him. It was a little like Malcolm's interception in Super Bowl XLIX: perfect timing and a bang-bang play. You had to tip your cap to the guy. He made a really good play and went 82 yards for the touchdown the other way to make it 21–0.

People wondered afterward if there was panic. Nope. Remember those games I wrote about in which we were in impossible spots and still won? New Orleans, Cleveland, Denver in 2013? The playoff games in 2014 against the Ravens and Seahawks? Almost coming back against Denver in the AFC Championship in 2015? It's the damn NFL. We weren't going to get blown out no matter what the scoreboard said. There are waves. You have to play in the waves and roll with them sometimes and let them do what they do. I was thinking that, believing in the best-case scenario at all times.

One more wave had to crash on our heads, though. We got a three-and-out and I had a twenty-six-yard punt return coming out of halftime. Soon we were facing third-and-12. We needed a play. The Falcons were in cover-5: two safeties split in zone coverage at the back of the defense and the corners playing man-to-man underneath. The area between the hash marks would be vacant. With the middle of the field open, I could make something happen.

I lined up wide right and Tom waved me in motion. When I reached the numbers, the ball was snapped. I beat the Falcons' corner Robert Alford by cutting in front of him "across his face," as we call it. The ball was there, waist high, as I crossed the middle. Perfect. All I wanted was to catch it and motor, because I knew I could lose Alford and turn it into a big gain. Instead, I dropped it.

We'd missed on a couple of plays in the first half, and I'd kept thinking then, *It's OK. Next play. On to the next play.* After that drop, though, I thought, *There aren't a lot of "next plays" left. I gotta help this team and start pulling my oar.*

The Falcons added another touchdown following that and it was 28–3 with 23:30 left in regulation. A little more than a point a minute to get even.

That's when Tom Brady became Tom Brady. After that touchdown, he jumped off the bench and stalked in front of the offense and said, "Let's go now! Let's go show some fight!" Right before we took the field, he said with the same urgency, "We gotta play *harder*! We gotta play *tougher*! Everything we *got*!" He was like a caged lion, pacing. I get chills just thinking about it now. He had that look in his eye. Dialed in.

You can ask people, "What quarterback would you want to have if you're down?" People might try to fight it and say Joe Montana, but after LI and seeing what Tom did? Seeing what he did against Seattle, seeing what he did against the Rams in his second year in the league? That's just legendary stuff. Legendary.

We answered back with a touchdown to make it 28–9 just before the end of the third. At that point, Dola, James White, Dion Lewis, and Hogan were balling out and Tom was working their matchups.

As the second half progressed and our comeback gained momentum, I didn't see any panic from the Falcons' defense. They were still playing hard; they weren't pointing fingers. We were on a mission and simply started playing better. We were in such a rhythm that I don't think it really mattered what defense was out there. We felt like we could go out and do what we needed to do.

I was proud of the way guys were rising to the occasion. Dola, playing in his hometown of Houston, was killing it. A tough, gritty dude who knows how to win ball games, he's the kind of guy you can count on in a big game, and he's shown that over and over for us. He reminds me a lot of Pops. He has a job, and he does it.

That comeback wasn't going to happen without our defense, though. They kept us afloat for a long time. Offensively, we gave Atlanta points in the first half, but the defense kept grinding. We were all confident in them, and I felt like something was going down at some point. Before Dont'a Hightower got that strip sack, I said on the bench, "We are going to get a fucking turnover here." I could feel it. And High made it happen. He's just a beast. A great leader and great playmaker. When Dola went in to make it 28–20 with five minutes left, I knew the defense would get it back for us.

It got a little hairy, though. A big catch-and-run to Devonta Freeman and Julio making a ridiculous catch on the sidelines got the ball down to our 22 with 4:47 left. Still, I was saying, "You gotta believe!" There's been a lot of discussion about the Falcons' playcalling on that drive after they got within field goal range. All I know is this: teams understand how well we play situational football. You can't take your foot off the pedal against us, because we keep coming. So it didn't surprise me that the Falcons kept throwing. They wanted to knock us out. Our defense wouldn't let them.

When we got the ball back, we needed a chunk play. We got it. I already explained how I saw "the catch" at the beginning of this book. Here's how TB saw that same twenty-three-yard completion on first-and-10 from our own 36.

Tom Brady

The route Jules ran was one he and I have worked on for a long time. When we run routes down the middle of the field, we usually feel that the bigger the target, the better. That's because big targets have a bigger catch radius. That's why when Gronk is in there, he gets the ball down the seam.

He's such a big target in the middle of the field that there is separation, from a quarterback's point of view. You can throw it higher than you would normally throw it.

When you put someone like Julian in there, who doesn't have the size, you gain some speed but you lose the ability to throw the ball high over the middle, because when you throw it higher over the middle, it gets intercepted. Those safeties back there are always waiting for the high throw—that's how a lot of them make the plays.

I threw that particular ball lower than I wanted to, and Robert Alford, the cornerback on Julian, did a good job getting his head around at the break point when Jules began his cut to the inside. He kind of shoved Julian into the break point, which threw Jules off and made him round the route a little bit. That's what a lot of good defensive backs do, and Alford is a veteran player. Jules came out of the turn stumbling a bit. Alford got his head around and I could sense that he was going to turn, so I tried to throw it quick but Alford got his hands on it.

Obviously, the ball was floating in the air and that was the game right there in many ways, what would happen in the next seconds. Jules had his feet under him enough so that he could really get to the ball by springing back toward it. They were playing the two-high defense, which meant both safeties were converging, so it was three on one. Normally those are bad numbers. But Julian just had incredible concentration in order for him to make that play.

After the replay challenge came back and it was first-and-10 at their 41, I knew we still had a lot to do, but I was juiced as we came to the line. I was across from Brian Poole, who I had debated with during the review. Just before the snap, I said, "See I told you I caught it. My bad!"

We still had our backs against the wall, but we had momentum, and things were falling our way. After the catch, my belief that we could potentially pull it off was even stronger. It was a crazy play that maybe should not have gone the way it did.

Then the ball was snapped and Dola got us another twenty yards. Two completions to James got us to their 1. James went in from there, then Tom hit Dola for the two-point conversion. Tied. With less than a minute left.

We won the coin toss before overtime—another nail in the Falcons' coffin. We'd scored 25 points in twenty-three minutes and we had Tom Brady and the best coaching staff in football. A touchdown meant the game was over. Anything less, and the Falcons would get the ball with a chance to win. We didn't plan on letting them touch it.

Before we took the field to start that last drive, I looked at Tom and said, "Let's go score and win this thing, baby."

"Let's go win it all," he answered.

"For your mom," I said. "For your mom."

Tom started OT the way he ended regulation: six yards to James, fourteen to Dola, eighteen to Hogan. We were across midfield. On a second-and-13 play, Tom found me on the left for fifteen to put us in field goal range. But when hadn't he come that far just to come that far! After James went around right end for ten yards, Tom tried to end it with a throw to Marty B. in the end zone. He drew the flag and we were on the doorstep, at the Falcons' 2. After an incompletion to Marty, James took it in from the 2.

My immediate thought? *Holy shit, we won!* But when I jumped on Tom, he said, "I don't think it's over yet, they have to review it." I felt a little wave of panic because the field was mobbed—our team, media, it was chaos. I thought we were going to get a penalty and be moved back to the 17, so I started screaming at everyone to get off the field. It wasn't until I saw Coach Belichick that I stopped freaking out. He was coming up to hug me and I said, "Is it over? They don't have to review it?" He went from a big smile to all business in a blink. "They reviewed it. We won." Then I just went crazy, jumping around, hugging everyone.

I found Tom and grabbed him in a tight hug. In that moment I realized that this quarterback—my quarterback—had just won his fifth Super Bowl. Nobody had ever done that.

"Five!" I said to Tom. "You've got five! I love you, bro!"

Looking back, I can see that my emotions after beating the Falcons were different from those when we beat the Seahawks. The comeback was ridiculous, so that's one. And the different things I'd gone through in my life since beating Seattle—having a kid, experiencing all that stress in the spring and learning how to manage it, the injuries—made this one special in a more personal way. So this time, I enjoyed it a little more. I exhaled. Sometimes I tend to be my own worst critic, picking apart everything I do. Sometimes I have to remind myself that it's going to be all right.

Sharing moments like that with my family is so special because I see how happy it makes them. During the season, I don't spend much time with them, and sometimes I can be an asshole because I'm so focused on what I have to do. It goes back to balance, how I feel I can't have it if I want to do well. Some people can, but I can't at this point in my life. At least, I don't think I can. So when I see my family, it makes me melt. I remember hugging my sister, Nicki, after the game and thinking about all she's accomplished and all she contributes as a fifth-grade teacher. At that point, I just wanted to tell her, "I love you and I'm proud of you." I just appreciated that she was there with me. It's kind of your time to put your guard down for a little while. For a short time, there's nothing else to get ready for. When you go out and achieve a goal, the ultimate goal, and you've got the people you love there and enjoying it with you, you're just happy.

Mom and Dad were there, and the hugs and tears flowed. I held on to Dad and wept. He whispered to me, "I know, son. Just hold on to Daddy."

"You gotta believe," I said into his shoulder.

He kissed my head and said, "You gotta believe."

More of my adult life has been spent in New England than the Bay Area. Redwood City will always be my hometown, but I don't know San Francisco like I know Boston. I don't know Lake Tahoe like I know the Cape. I'm here nine months of the year now. If you put the numbers behind it, even though I've got that California swag, I'm a New Englander.

The Patriots are the team that gave me my shot; this is the team that I grew up with and this is where I belong. In June 2017, I signed a contract extension that will keep me with the Patriots through 2019. It took a long time to negotiate. That's not a surprise: contracts with the Patriots take a long time and I'm a thirty-one-year-old wide receiver in the NFL who will be thirty-three when the contract ends. The team had its considerations and we had ours. One of the biggest for me was Boston.

I get to play in a Patriots uniform for my ninth year. It's pretty cool to play somewhere as long as I have for owners like the Kraft family, for the best coach to ever blow a whistle, and for the best quarterback of all time. It's a good situation to be in. It's the fans, too. They're the best in the country. This is a pro-sports city. You can talk about Chicago and New

York, but those are huge-ass places. Boston's small, and that means the intensity is that much higher. There's nowhere to hide from it, and I like it like that. That's why I live right downtown now, in the heart of the city.

Social media has become a big part of my connecting with fans directly. Football comes first, but that doesn't mean I don't have a creative side, a part that wants to make and imagine. My friend Assaf Swissa and I started making videos and posting pictures a few years ago, and after a little while it built a life of its own. Assaf can talk about our social media statistics and all the awards we've won—but it's all for fun. The fans in New England are so receptive—they empower us to continue making content we love to make.

In June 2017, I shared a letter that my English professor from the College of San Mateo sent me. So much time has passed, I don't remember exactly what happened in her class-room in 2005, but apparently, I mentioned trying to play "in the league." The professor told me to set more realistic goals. Twelve years later, she took the time to write me and apologize for being "flippant." I was honored and thought it was worth sharing with everyone because, she's right, those dreams we're chasing need to be cultivated, not stepped on. But it's also important to be able to say to someone, "I got this wrong. I'm sorry."

I know I get to do incredibly cool things and, to me, shar-ing those things lets people know how much I appreciate it. If I didn't like to share, would I have done that naked photo shoot for ESPN in the spring of 2017? Five hours, completely bare.

People wanting to see you naked is a perk of the job. Or wanting to see you dressed up, which I love doing and always have. Believe me, if I didn't have the platform I do, I wouldn't have the chance to dress like this. I look at these opportunities as on-the-job training for whatever's next. Merchandise we create, market, and sell on my website or the social media content we make is about reading tastes and passions, then marketing to them.

There's no one more valuable for me to learn from than Tom and his wife, Gisele Bündchen, in a lot of ways. Every time I'm around them, I learn. The way they are with their kids, the way they make time to spend with each other, they are just good people. Tom's stuck with me through some hard times, and he's always shown real concern about me doing the right things. How could I be luckier than that? Gisele is just very caring. She knows what's up in my life and she asks and listens. She's a really free spirit, and being around them with their vibe is comforting. They've seen me grow from the kid who'd eat lunch at their house in LA after a workout to someone who spends big chunks of time with them in Montana. It's a true and genuine relationship.

I would love to have a relationship like theirs, but living with me right now would be tough for anyone. Dating isn't easy. I have Lily, I've got business interests, and when it's the football season, I don't have time to sit and check in every day with someone. You have to be ready to give your partner that time, and right now, it's a challenge for me. The next year of my life is already scheduled out. I would love to be in a relationship sooner rather than later, but I just have to find the right person, and right now my life is about football and my child.

When Dad stopped playing in a rock band and was done chasing that dream, he devoted himself to his family. I would love to do the same thing—just without driving a 1991 Suburban and wearing sweatpants, a fanny pack, and six-year-old Pumas. I want to still have my fun, though. Dad thinks that when he's sitting on the couch, he's saving money. Mom wants to get out there and have fun. As I said, I have a little more Angie in me, I think.

One thing I've explored that my family didn't is our Jew-ish heritage. I used to describe myself as Jew-ish, as in I knew that "Edelman" was a Jewish name, but I wasn't really in touch with the faith. But I've always been interested in where I came from, and a few years back, I went on Ancestry.com and researched back through my paternal grandfather.

What got me more involved was a chance meeting I had in an LA restaurant with a guy I met through mutual friends, Erik Litmanovich. I was introduced to him and he didn't even say hello. He said, "Are you Jewish?" I said, "Well, my grandfather was, but I don't really know. I didn't practice it growing up."

This guy then starts rattling off all my stats from the Patriots, all my stats from Kent. He'd been following me since college because of my last name. We began to form a friend-ship, and he introduced me to Rabbi Yossi in Los Angeles, who I pray with every Friday during the season by phone. Between Erik and David Rosenberg, a friend of mine from Swampscott, Massachusetts, who owns the Prime Auto deal-ership, I've gotten more attuned to the religion and history. During the 2014 NFL season, the Israeli ambassador to the United States, Ron Dermer, was in our locker room as a guest of Mr. Kraft and put a US-Israeli pin on my hat. I wore it the rest of the season and things went well for us. In June 2015, Mr. Kraft helped set me up on a trip to the Holy Land. It was incredibly moving to feel the history and meet the people in Israel. They are so full of life and faith even though there's a lot of hate for them. There's a lot to admire about them. Now, when I see Mr. Kraft on Friday, I'll say, "*Shabbat shalom.*"

One word that attracts me is *avodah*, which is the Hebrew word for work. A rabbi told me that we are put on Earth to work, and that working hard is honoring who you are and your family and God. That is an important idea for me.

My family is kind of amused by all the Jewish-awakening stuff. We weren't religious at all, so they wonder what's going on. I'll try to push them to explore it and they'll say, "We don't know anything about this!" and I'll say, "Well, why don't we just start?" But it's a personal decision. It's faith. I still think Dad practices *avodah* every day, though.

It's important to take stock of where you are in life. Are you growing as a person? Are you achieving goals? Are you living a life that's a good example? Now that I'm a father, I'm even more conscious of that. Obviously, everyone makes mistakes, and I've made plenty. But I also think I've lived the American dream. I've had to be persistent and relentless to achieve the goals I set and reach my potential. That's the American dream, isn't it? To realize what you can truly be?

I'm not done yet. Neither are the guys I'm with. In early July, we went up to Tom's house in Montana for a few days, and he put us through what he likes to call "Gladiator Camp." I call it "Fat Kid Camp," because he never lets us stop. Six days in a row, we're up there running forty or fifty routes for him, then golfing for four hours then riding ATVs, then dinner; it's insane. He plans everything out for the whole week, and prints schedules out and gives them to everyone. I'm like, "Bro, I need no plans. Let's train and whatever comes, comes!" Tom doesn't do it that way.

I honestly don't think he'll ever slow down. As for me, I don't know how long I will play, but I intend to keep going until the wheels fall off and my body says "You're done." Even after we do stop—and neither Tom nor I has a plan for that—what will we do? Play slow-pitch softball? Or maybe we can coach together if his kids play football. I can be just like that old Pop Warner legend, Coach Edelman.

ACKNOWLEDGMENTS

FROM JULIAN EDELMAN

The greatest gifts in life come from family. Nicki, your love and unconditional support is humbling and sustaining. Jason, your resilience and loyalty is inspiring and dependable. Mom and Dad, you had nothing but gave me everything. Thank you.

Lily, the world is so much bigger now that you are in it. I love you.

You have my love and gratitude, Mr. Kraft. Jonathan and Danny Kraft, I value the relationships we've built, and I will always honor your mother. Thank you, Mrs. Kraft.

To all my coaches at every stop, especially Coach Belichick. Scotty O and Chaddy O, thanks for sticking with me.

To Don Yee, Carter Chow, Steve Dubin, and everyone at Yee and Dubin Sports—I know you always have my back!

Superdigital, thanks for helping me discover my creative side. Assaf, *todah achi*.

To the unbelievable fans of New England, thank you for an amazing ride.

FROM TOM E. CURRAN

Thanks first to my friend Michael Holley for both putting me in touch with Mauro DiPreta at Hachette Books and for listening to my sniveling as the project moved forward at warp speed.

I also want to send my thanks to Mauro for providing the requisite editorial kick in the ass or pat on the back depending on the day, and to the rest of the team at Hachette Books for making this book as great as it could be. My *Boston Sports Tonight* crew deserve a medal for putting up with my paper-thin nerves all summer, as does my guy Phil Perry, who kept the Patriots beat on lock. I am also grateful to my bosses at CSN New England—Kevin Miller and Princell Hair—who heard me out on this book and said, "Do it." And I want to extend my thanks to Jayde Huxtable, Hannah Chapman, and Tess Rowland for the life-saving transcription work.

To all of Jules's coaches, teammates, and friends—especially those in the Patriots organization including Bill Belichick, Tom Brady, Robert and Jonathan Kraft, and Stacey James—thank you for being open and available. It's been a privilege to cover the unprecedented success of this team, and I appreciate each of the friendships that we have developed throughout the process. Once I realized I wouldn't play in the NFL, I knew I wanted to cover it. I know how lucky I've been to be ringside since 1997 for the best show in sports.

A big thanks goes out to Frank, Angie, and Nicki Edelman. Thank you for all your candor and support throughout the summer. To my parents, Frank and Jane, and my brother, Mike: Thank you for giving me a love for reading, and for teaching me that you gotta do what you gotta do when you gotta do it.

I am beyond lucky to have in my three sons, Sam, Dan, and Tim, my three role models. And all my love goes out to the real MVP, my wife, Erica. You are truly the "greatest catch ever."